INSECT LITERATURE

Insect Literature

by

Lafcadio Hearn

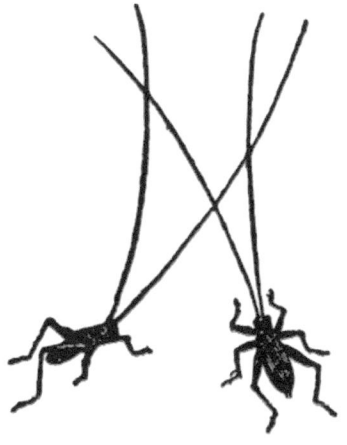

The Swan River Press
Dublin, Ireland
MMXX

Insect Literature
by Lafcadio Hearn

Published by
The Swan River Press
Dublin, Ireland
in October, MMXX

www.swanriverpress.ie
brian@swanriverpress.ie

"Of Insects and Children" © Anne-Sylvie Homassel, MMXV
This edition © Swan River Press, MMXV

Dust jacket and cover design by Meggan Kehrli
from "Bug" © Takato Yamamoto/Uptight Co. Ltd, MMV

Interior illustrations from *Exotics and Retrospectives* (1898),
A Japanese Miscellany (1901), *Shadowings* (1901),
and *Kottō* (1902).

Set in Garamond by Ken Mackenzie

Paperback Edition
ISBN 978-1-78380-740-6

Swan River Press published a limited edition
hardback of *Insect Literature* in October 2015.

目次
Contents

Of Insects and Children *Anne-Sylvie Homassel*	. . . . .	vii
Foreword *Masanobu Ōtani*	. . . .	xiii

Insect Literature

I.	Butterflies	. . . .	1
II.	Mosquitoes	. . . . . .	19
III.	Ants	. . . .	23
IV.	Story of a Fly	. . . . .	41
V.	Fireflies	. . . . . .	45
VI.	Dragon-flies	. . . . .	71
VII.	Sémi	. . . .	103
VIII.	Insect-Musicians	. . . .	129
IX.	Kusa-Hibari	. . . . .	157

X.	Some Poems about Insects	163
XI.	Insects and Greek Poetry	202
XII.	Some French Poetry about Insects	214
XIII.	Insect Politics	234
XIV.	Under the Electric Light	236
XV.	——! ——!! Mosquitoes!!!	238
XVI.	The Festive	240
XVII.	The Jewel Insect	242
XVIII.	Dr. Hava's Tarantula	243
XIX.	Gaki	248
XX.	The Dream of Akinosuké	262
Acknowledgements		270
About the Author		273

蟲と子供達について
Of Insects and Children

In February 1920, the Hokuseidō publishing house in Tōkyō commenced with its bilingual "Hearn Memorial Translations". The nine-volume series showcased a broad selection of Lafcadio Hearn's work: from diaries and letters to essays and stories; the texts appeared in English followed by the corresponding Japanese translations on the opposite pages. The fifth book in the series was a selection of ten essays on insects, translated and annotated by one of Hearn's former pupils, Masanobu Ōtani (1875-1933). The resulting volume, *Insect Literature*, was published on 27 February 1921. Just months after the ninth volume, an expanded edition of *Kwaidan*, was published in March 1923, the "Hearn Memorial Translations" series abruptly went out of print when a fire caused by the Great Kantō earthquake in September 1923 destroyed Hokuseidō's entire stock.

"Lafcadio Hearn was very fond of insects," wrote Ōtani in his foreword to *Insect Literature*. "Naturally he wrote much about them; there are, I believe, few writers either in the East or the West who wrote so much and so beautifully on insects as he." Ōtani himself had contributed to the inception of some of these essays: as a young man he worked as Hearn's research assistant, providing the author with a great wealth of literary and descriptive sources on the insects of Japan. Together with other students, Ōtani also facilitated the handover of some of Hearn's lecture notebooks to John Erskine, an editor and professor of English at Columbia University. From this material, Erskine was able to edit and publish Hearn's lessons at the Imperial University of Tōkyō, three of which dealt with insects and poetry: "Some Poems about Insects", "Insects and Greek Poetry", and "Some French Poetry about Insects" are, of course, included in the present collection—although the latter two were not in the original edition of *Insect Literature*.

Lafcadio Hearn was interested in insects well before he came to Japan. Born to a Greek mother and an Irish father on the Ionian island of Lefkada in 1850, he was reared in Dublin by his great-aunt Mrs. Sarah Brenane, and finished his formal education at a boarding school in England. Hearn's mother Rosa had left Dublin and returned to Greece when Lafcadio was only four years old, while his father, Surgeon-Major Charles Hearn, had married his childhood love and pursued his military career in India, leaving his two sons from his first marriage in Europe.

Biographer Paul Murray notes the "romantic fog" Hearn created around his early years. At the age of nineteen, Lafcadio was sent to the United States by his great-aunt. According to Hearn, after some years of poverty and hardship—doing anything by which he could "turn an honest dollar"—he eventually settled in Cincinnati where he became a journalist. Edward Laroque Tinker published in 1924 *Lafcadio Hearn's American Days*, a somewhat prudish account of Hearn's adventures in America. The coy biographer often leaves his subject to speak for himself on topics deemed too shocking. Thus the reader has the pleasure to read in full Hearn's essay on "The Sexual Idea in French Literature", which includes a few lines on Jules Michelet, "the historian of Sexual Af-

Of Insects and Children

fection". Hearn wrote, "After perusing his works, *La Mer*, *L'Oiseau*, *L'Insecte*—especially, perhaps, the last, in which we read so wonderful a history of the republican ants and monarchical bees, one feels the great tenderness of the man to all living creatures entering into himself. A friend told us not very long ago that, after reading the book, he could never find the courage to kill either an ant or a spider." The article was published in the *New Orleans Item* (17 June 1881). Hearn was then living amongst the mosquitoes and cockroaches in the swamp-like climate of that city and, as his "Dr. Hava's Tarantula" attests, with its monstrous wasps, scorpions, and spiders; he did not always display a similar kindness towards the creatures of the crawling order. However, a few years later in 1885, Hearn was to marvel at the Japanese fabrics displayed in the pavilions of the Exhibition of New Orleans and at the fabulous snakes and bugs their patterns depicted.

Settling in Japan in 1890, Hearn was freer to express his love of insects, as literary objects and creations of nature—no lesser beings than animals or men. Such was their place in Japan, as he could now observe. They were petted, they were sung, they were part of the Buddhist cosmogony. In his essay on *gaki* (added to the contents of the present edition), Hearn explains that the Gakidō, the last world before the Jigokudō, the Buddhist hell, houses many insects which are reincarnations of human beings. The Gakidō is separated from the Ningendō, the world of humans, by the Chikushōdō, the world of the animals, and the Shuradō, the world of battles and slaughters. Some *gaki*—the *gaki-sekai-jū*—remain in the Gakidō; others—called *nin-chū-jū*—live amongst men, sometimes in the shape of insects. In "Gaki", Hearn somewhat distances himself from the Buddhist classification: however, he acknowledges its relevance when it comes to his own conception of insects, the very nature of which appear to him as entomologically and supernaturally significant. Insects are wonderful beings in every sense of the word, and they have a close connection with the human race: "Whether *gaki* do or do not exist, there is at least some shadowing of truth in the Eastern belief that the dead become insects." Concluding this essay, Hearn pictures his reincarnated self as a "Wind-eater", or as an *amembo*, a skater; or rather a *sémi* (a Japanese cicada), or a dragon-fly. "In fact, I have not been able to convince myself that it is really an inestimable privilege to be reborn a human being."

In his essay "Mosquitoes", which the reader will also find in the following pages, Hearn amusingly considers a rebirth as a buzzing pest: "And, considering the possibility of being doomed to the state of a *jiki-ketsu-gaki* (a blood-sucking *gaki*), I want to have my chance of being reborn in some bamboo flower-cup, or *mizutamé*, whence I might issue softly, singing my thin and pungent song, to bite some people that I know."

According to Hearn, it is because Japan, as a Buddhist land, includes insects in the order of the world, while still acknowledging their unsettling uncanniness, that its poets have often sung of them, as the Greeks did two millennia before. Insects are loved, hunted—not to be killed, but to be kept as pets—sometimes bred, as is the case with musical insects; they assume in the Japanese poetry the same aurally vibrant and visually vivid presence that they display in the Japanese landscape. In his essays on butterflies, on *sémi*, on dragon-flies, on fire-flies, and on musical insects, Hearn mixes with the descriptions of these species many Japanese poems, mostly *haiku*, collected by his students. So too are Hearn's descriptions more poetical than entomological, the author being more concerned with the strange qualities of the bugs, or with their songs, or with

Of Insects and Children

the anthropomorphic associations they trigger than he is in decidedly more scientific contemplations.

Masanobu Ōtani's original selection for *Insect Literature* included only ten essays and stories, and he arranged the contents according to the seasons in which the insects treated appear. However the final piece in the 1921 edition, "Some Poems about Insects", mentions a variety of insects and allows Hearn to disconnect himself from the literary tradition of the West and the Christian influence that he deems responsible for the anthropocentrism of its arts and literature. "What is the signification of the great modern silence in Western countries upon this delightful topic? I believe that Christianity, as dogma, accounts for the long silence. The opinions of the early Church refused soul, ghost, intelligence of any sort to other creatures than man".

To this new edition of *Insect Literature*, we have added a further ten insect-related pieces that were not in the original volume. In the first of these, "Insects and Greek Poetry", Hearn, seemingly closing the full circle of his own destiny, underlines the kinship between the Japanese and the Greek perceptions of the world of insects—and of the world at large: " . . . it should be interesting to the Japanese student of literature to know that his own people accord with the old Greeks in their appreciation of insect music as one of the great charms of country life", explains Hearn, a parallel further developed in the course of the essay. "It was not only in writing about insects that the Greek poets came close to the Japanese poets: they came close to them also in a thousand little touches of an emotional kind, referring to the gods, the fate of man, the pleasure of festival days, those sorrows of existence which have been the same in all ages of humanity."

The similitude is eerily and touchingly illustrated by the echoing presence in Hearn's essays on insects of dead or grieving children: both the young Myro, sung by Anyte of Sicilia, and the Japanese girl in "Sémi" mourn the demise of their pet insects; in "Insects and Greek Poetry", the infant son of the poet Okura is too little to walk all the way to the realm of the dead, just as Cynirus's son, crossing the Styx, must be carried out of Charon's boat. And in the pages which follow, the reader might well hear the spectral laughter of many insect-hunting children going joyfully about their task. Hearn's engagement with Japan and its insect culture is not wholly fanciful. He lived there, got married and had children there, and was buried in Tōkyō under the Japanese name Koizumi Yakumo (小泉八雲)—even though he never really mastered the language. But there may be, in Hearn's fantasised Japan, the trappings of a childhood country, desirable, innocent, mirthful, and sometimes terrifying, of which the insects are the splendid and monstrous incarnation.

Anne-Sylvie Homassel
Arcueil, France
July 2015

はしがき
Foreword

Lafcadio Hearn was very fond of insects. Naturally he wrote much about them; there are, I believe, few writers either in the East or in the West who wrote so much and so beautifully about insects as he.

This is a collection of all the essays, stories, and lectures concerning insects among his works. Apart from his fluent and elegant style, I am sure, the reader will find the thought of his articles very interesting and will be astonished to know how he made the best use in his works of Japanese poems, many of which are perhaps unfamiliar even to the Japanese reader.

For the benefit of English students I have put literal translations on the pages opposite the original, together with some annotations. But I must ask the Japanese reader to study the original with much care and to try to appreciate the charms of Hearn's English for himself.

I must also say in justice to Hearn that, as it was I who furnished him with the materials for nearly all the articles contained in this book, I am responsible for the mistakes, if there be any, in the descriptions of Japanese insects and in the quotations from poems or other records relating to insects.

The contents of this book are not arranged chronologically but according to the seasons in which the insects treated appear.

Insect Literature

"Butterflies", "Mosquitoes", and "Ants" from *Kwaidan* (1904); "Story of a Fly" and "Fireflies" from *Kottō* (1902); "Dragon-flies" from *A Japanese Miscellany* (1901); "Sémi" from *Shadowings* (1900); "Insect-Musicians" from *Exotics and Retrospectives* (1898); "Kusa-Hibari" from *Kottō* and "Some Poems about Insects" from *Interpretations of Literature* (1915). The last named work is, by the bye, one of the books which Prof. J. Erskine edited after Hearn's death, by synthesising the note-book records of Hearn's lectures in the Tōkyō Imperial University taken by certain classmates of mine and myself.

Masanobu Ōtani
Kanazawa, Japan
November 1920

Insect Literature

蝶
Butterflies

I.

Would that I could hope for the luck of that Chinese scholar known to Japanese literature as "Rōsan"! For he was beloved by two spirit-maidens, celestial sisters, who every ten days came to visit him and to tell him stories about butterflies. Now there are marvellous Chinese stories about butterflies—ghostly stories; and I want to know them. But never shall I be able to read Chinese, nor even Japanese; and the little Japanese poetry that I manage, with exceeding difficulty, to translate, contains so many allusions to Chinese stories of butterflies that I am tormented with the torment of Tantalus . . . And, of course, no spirit-maidens will ever deign to visit so sceptical a person as myself.

I want to know, for example, the whole story of that Chinese maiden whom the butterflies took to be a flower, and followed in multitude—so fragrant and so fair was she. Also I should like to know something more concerning the butterflies of the Emperor Gensō, or Ming Hwang, who made them choose his loves for him . . . He used to hold wine-parties in his amazing garden; and ladies of exceeding beauty were in attendance; and caged butterflies, set free among them, would fly to the fairest; and then, upon that fairest the Imperial favour was bestowed. But after Gensō Kōtei had seen Yōkihi (whom the Chinese call Yang-Kwei-Fei), he would not suffer the butterflies to choose for him—which was unlucky, as Yōkihi got him into serious trouble . . . Again, I should like to know more about the experience of that Chinese scholar, celebrated in Japan under the name of Sōshū, who dreamed that he was a butterfly, and had all the sensations of a butterfly in that dream. For his spirit had really been wandering about in the shape of a butterfly; and, when he awoke, the memories and the feelings of butterfly existence remained so vivid in his mind that he could not act like a human being . . . Finally I should like to know the text of a certain Chinese official recognition of sundry butterflies as the spirits of an Emperor and of his attendants . . .

Most of the Japanese literature about butterflies, excepting some poetry, appears to be of Chinese origin; and even that old national aesthetic feeling on the subject, which found such delightful expression in Japanese art and song and custom, may have been first developed under Chinese teaching. Chinese precedent doubtless explains why Japanese poets and painters chose so often for their *Geimyō*, or professional appellations, such names as *Chōmu* (Butterfly-Dream), *Ichō* (Solitary Butterfly), etc. And even to this day such *geimyō* as *Chōhana* (Butterfly-Blossom), *Chōkichi* (Butterfly-Luck), or *Chōnosuké* (Butterfly-Help) are affected by dancing-girls. Besides artistic names having reference to butterflies, there are still in use real personal names (*yobina*) of this kind—such as *Kochō*, or *Chō*, meaning "Butterfly". They are borne by women only, as a rule—though there are some strange exceptions . . . And here I may mention that, in the province of Mutsu, there still exists the curious old custom of calling the youngest daughter in a family *Tekona*—which quaint word, obsolete elsewhere, signifies in Mutsu dialect a butterfly. In classic time this word signified also a beautiful woman . . .

It is possible also that some weird Japanese beliefs about butterflies are of Chinese derivation; but these beliefs might be older than China herself. The most interesting one, I think, is that the soul of a *living* person may wander about in the form of a butterfly. Some pretty fancies have been evolved out of this belief—such as the notion that if a butterfly enters your guest-room and perches behind the bamboo screen, the person whom you most love is coming to see you. That a butterfly may be the spirit of somebody is not a reason for being afraid of it. Nevertheless there are times when even butterflies can inspire fear by appearing in prodigious numbers; and Japanese history records such an event. When Taīra-no-Masakado was secretly preparing for his famous revolt, there appeared in Kyōto so vast a swarm of butterflies that the people were frightened—thinking the apparition to be a portent of coming evil . . . Perhaps those butterflies were supposed to be the spirits of the thousands doomed to perish in battle, and agitated on the eve of war by some mysterious premonition of death.

However, in Japanese belief, a butterfly may be the soul of a dead person as well as of a living person. Indeed it is a custom of souls to take butterfly-shape in order to announce the fact of their final departure from the body; and for this reason any butterfly which enters a house ought to be kindly treated.

To this belief, and to queer fancies connected with it, there are many allusions in popular drama. For example, there is a well-known play called *Tondédéru-Kochō-no-Kanza-shi*; or, *The Flying Hairpin of Kochō*. Kochō is a beautiful person who kills herself because of false accusations and cruel treatment. Her would-be avenger long seeks in vain for the author of the wrong. But at last the dead woman's hairpin turns into a butterfly, and serves as a guide to vengeance by hovering above the place where the villain is hiding.

Of course those big paper butterflies (*o-chō* and *me-chō*) which figure at weddings must not be thought of as having any ghostly signification. As emblems they only express the joy of loving union, and the hope that the newly married couple may pass through life together as a pair of butterflies flit lightly through some pleasant garden—now hovering upward, now downward, but never widely separating.

II.

A small selection of *hokku* on butterflies will help to illustrate Japanese interest in the aesthetic side of the subject. Some are pictures only—tiny colour sketches made with seventeen syllables; some are nothing more than pretty fancies, or graceful suggestions;—but the reader will find variety. Probably he will not care much for the verses in themselves. The taste for Japanese poetry of the epigrammatic sort is a taste that must be slowly acquired; and it is only by degrees, after patient study, that the possibilities of such composition can be fairly estimated. Hasty criticism has declared that to put forward any serious claim on behalf of seventeen-syllable poems "would be absurd". But what, then, of Crashaw's famous line upon the miracle at the marriage feast in Cana?—

Nympha pudica Deum vidit, et erubuit.[1]

Only fourteen syllables—and immortality. Now with seventeen Japanese syllables things quite as wonderful—indeed, much more wonderful—have been done, not once or twice, but probably a thousand times . . . However, there is nothing wonderful in the following *hokku*, which have been selected for more than literary reasons:—

Nugi-kakuru[2]
 Haori sugata no
  Kochō kana!

(Like a *haori* being taken off—that is the shape of a butterfly!)

Torisashi no
 Sao no jama suru,
  Kochō kana!

(Ah, the butterfly keeps getting in the way of the bird-catcher's pole![3])

Tsurigané ni
 Tomarité nemuru
  Kochō kana!

(Perched upon the temple-bell, the butterfly sleeps!)

Néru-uchi mo
 Asobu-yumé wo ya—
  Kusa no chō!

(Even while sleeping, its dream is of play—ah, the butterfly of the grass![4])

Oki, oki yo!
　Waga tomo ni sen,
　　Néru-kochō!

(Wake up! Wake up!—I will make thee my comrade, thou sleeping butterfly.[5])

Kago no tori
　Chō wo urayamu
　　Metsuki kana!

(Ah, the sad expression in the eyes of that caged bird!—envying the butterfly!)

Chō tondé—
　Kazé naki hi to mo
　　Miëzari ki!

(Even though it did not appear to be a windy day,[6] the fluttering of the butterflies—!)

Rakkwa éda ni
　Kaëru to miréba—
　　Kochō kana!

(When I saw the fallen flower return to the branch—lo! it was only a butterfly![7])

Chiru-hana ni—
　Karusa arasoü
　　Kochō kana!

(How the butterfly strives to compete in lightness with the falling flowers![8])

Butterflies

Chōchō ya!
  Onna no michi no
    Ato ya saki!
(See that butterfly on the woman's path—now fluttering behind her, now before!)

Chōchō ya!
  Hana-nusubito wo
    Tsukété-yuku!

(Ha! The butterfly!—it is following the person who stole the flowers!)

Aki no chō
  Tomo nakéréba ya;
    Hito ni tsuku.

(Poor autumn butterfly!—when left without a comrade [of its own race], it follows after man [or "a person"]!)

Owarété mo,
  Isoganu furi no
    Chōchō kana!

(Ah, the butterfly! Even when chased, it never has the air of being in a hurry.)

Chō wa mina
  Jiu-shichi-hachi no
    Sugata kana!

(As for butterflies, they all have the appearance of being about seventeen or eighteen years old.[9])

Chō tobu ya—
 Kono yo no urami
  Naki yō ni!
(How the butterfly sports,—just as if there were no enmity [or "envy"] in this world!)

Chō tobu ya,
 Kono yo ni nozomi,
  Nai yō ni!

(Ah, the butterfly!—it sports about as if it had nothing more to desire in this present state of existence.)

Nami no hana ni
 Tomari kanétaru,
  Kochō kana!

(Having found it difficult indeed to perch upon the [foam-] blossoms of the waves—alas for the butterfly!)

Mutsumashi ya!—
 Umaré-kawaraba
  Nobé no chō.[10]

(If [in our next existence] we be born into the state of butterflies upon the moor, then perchance we may be happy together!)

Nadéshiko ni
 Chōchō shiroshi—
  Taré no kon?[11]

(On the pink-flower there is a white butterfly: whose spirit, I wonder?)

Butterflies

Ichi-nichi no
  Tsuma to miëkéri—
    Chō futatsu.

(The one-day wife has at last appeared—a pair of butterflies!)

Kité wa maü,
  Futari shidzuka no
    Kochō kana!

(Approaching they dance; but when the two meet at last they are very quiet, the butterflies!)

Chō wo oü
  Kokoro-mochitashi
    Itsumadémo!

(Would that I might always have the heart [desire] of chasing butterflies![12])

Besides these specimens of poetry about butterflies, I have one queer example to offer of Japanese prose literature on the same topic. The original, of which I have attempted only a free translation, can be found in the curious old book *Mushi-Isame* ("Insect-Admonitions"); and it assumes the form of a discourse to a butterfly. But it is really a didactic allegory—suggesting the moral significance of a social rise and fall:—

"Now, under the sun of spring, the winds are gentle, and flowers pinkly bloom, and grasses are soft, and the hearts of people are glad. Butterflies everywhere flutter joyously: so many persons now compose Chinese verses and Japanese verses about butterflies.

"And this season, O Butterfly, is indeed the season of your bright prosperity: so comely you now are that in the whole world there is nothing more comely. For that reason all other insects admire and envy you;—there is not among them even one that does not envy you. Nor do insects alone regard you with envy: men also both envy and admire you. Sōshū of China, in a dream, assumed your shape;—Sakoku of Japan, after dying, took your form, and therein made ghostly apparition. Nor is the envy that you inspire shared only by insects and mankind: even things without soul change their form into yours;—witness the barley-grass, which turns into a butterfly.[13]

"And therefore you are lifted up with pride, and think to yourself: 'In all this world there is nothing superior to me!' Ah! I can very well guess what is in your heart: you are too much satisfied with your own person. That is why you let yourself be blown thus lightly about by every wind;—that is why you never remain still,—always, always thinking: 'In the whole world there is no one so fortunate as I.'

"But now try to think a little about your own personal history. It is worth recalling; for there is a vulgar side to it. How a vulgar side? Well, for a considerable time after you were born, you had no such reason for rejoicing in your form. You were then a mere cabbage-insect, a hairy worm; and you were so poor that you could not afford even one robe to cover your nakedness; and your appearance was altogether disgusting. Everybody in those days hated the sight of you. Indeed you had good reason to be ashamed of yourself; and so ashamed you were that you collected old twigs and rubbish to hide in, and you made a hiding-nest, and hung it to a branch,—and then everybody cried out at you, 'Raincoat Insect!' (*Minomushi*).[14] And during that period of your life, your sins were grievous. Among the tender green leaves of beautiful cherry-trees you and your fellows assembled, and there made ugliness extraordinary; and the expectant eyes of the people, who came from far away to admire the beauty of those cherry-trees, were hurt by the sight of you. And of things even more hateful than this you were guilty. You knew that poor, poor men and women had been cultivating *daikon* in their fields—toiling and toiling under the hot sun till their hearts were filled with bitterness by reason of having to care for that *daikon*; and you persuaded your companions to go with you, and to gather upon the leaves of that *daikon*, and on the leaves of other vegetables planted by those poor people. Out of your greediness you ravaged those leaves, and gnawed them into all shapes of ugliness—caring nothing for the trouble of those poor folk . . . Yes, such a creature you were, and such were your doings.

"And now that you have a comely form, you despise your old comrades, the insects; and, whenever you happen to meet any of them, you pretend not to know them (literally, "You make an I-don't-know face"). Now you want to have none but wealthy and exalted people for friends . . . Ah! you have forgotten the old times, have you?

"It is true that many people have forgotten your past, and are charmed by the sight of your present graceful shape and white wings, and write Chinese verses and Japanese verses about you. The high-born damsel, who could not bear even to look at you in your former shape, now gazes at you with delight, and wants you to perch upon her hairpin, and holds out her dainty fan in the hope that you will light upon it. But this reminds me that there is an ancient Chinese story about you, which is not pretty.

"In the time of the Emperor Gensō, the Imperial Palace contained hundreds and thousands of beautiful ladies, so many, indeed, that it would have been difficult for any man to decide which among them was the loveliest. So all of those beautiful persons were assembled together in one place; and you were set free to fly among them; and it was decreed that the damsel upon whose hairpin you perched should be augustly summoned to the Imperial Chamber. In that time there could not be more than one Empress—which was a good law; but, because of you, the Emperor Gensō did great mischief in the land. For your mind is light and frivolous; and although among so many beautiful women there must have been some persons of pure heart, you would look for nothing but beauty, and so betook yourself to the person most beautiful in outward appearance. Therefore many of the female attendants ceased altogether to think about the right way of women, and began to study how to make themselves appear splendid in the eyes of men. And the end of it was that the Emperor Gensō died a pitiful and painful death—all because of your light and trifling mind. Indeed, your real character can easily be seen from your conduct in other matters. There are trees, for example—such as the evergreen-oak and the pine—whose leaves do not fade· and fall, but remain always green;—these are trees of firm heart, trees of solid character. But you say that they are stiff and formal; and you hate the sight of them, and never pay them a visit. Only to the cherry-tree, and the *kaido*,[15] and the peony, and the yellow rose you go: those you like because they have showy flowers, and you try only to please them. Such conduct, let me assure you, is very unbecoming. Those trees certainly have handsome flowers; but hunger-satisfying fruits they have not; and they are grateful to those only who are fond of luxury and show. And that is just the reason why they are pleased by your fluttering wings and delicate shape;—that is why they are kind to you.

"Now, in this spring season, while you sportively dance through the gardens of the wealthy, or hover among the beautiful alleys of cherry-trees in blossom, you say to yourself: 'Nobody in the world has such pleasure as I, or such excellent friends. And, in spite of all that people may say, I most love the peony,—and the golden yellow rose is my own darling, and I will obey her every least behest; for that is my pride and my delight.' . . . So you say. But the opulent and elegant season of flowers is very short: soon they will fade and fall. Then, in the time of summer heat, there will be green leaves only; and presently the winds of autumn will blow, when even the leaves themselves will shower down like rain, *parari-parari*. And your fate will then be as the fate of the unlucky in the proverb, '*Tanomi ki no shita ni amé furu*' (Even through the tree on which I relied for shelter the rain leaks down). For you will seek out your old friend, the root-cutting insect, the grub, and beg him to let you return into your old-time hole;— but now having wings, you will not be able to enter the hole because of them, and you will not be able to shelter your body anywhere between heaven and earth, and all the moor-grass will then have withered, and you will not have even one drop of dew with which to moisten your tongue,—and there will be nothing left for you to do but to lie down and die. All because of your light and frivolous heart—but, ah! how lamentable an end! . . . "

III.

Most of the Japanese stories about butterflies appear, as I have said, to be of Chinese origin. But I have one which is probably indigenous; and it seems to me worth telling for the benefit of persons who believe that there is no "romantic love" in the Far East.

Behind the cemetery of the temple of Sōzanji, in the suburbs of the capital, there long stood a solitary cottage, occupied by an old man named Takahama. He was liked in the neighbourhood, by reason of his amiable ways; but almost everybody supposed him to be a little mad. Unless a man take the Buddhist vows, he is expected to marry, and to bring up a family. But Takahama did not belong to the religious life; and he could not be persuaded to marry. Neither had he ever been known to enter in to a love-relation with any woman. For more than fifty years he had lived entirely alone.

One summer he fell sick, and knew that he had not long to live. He then sent for his sister-in-law, a widow, and for her only son—a lad of about twenty years old, to whom he was much attached. Both promptly came, and did whatever they could to soothe the old man's last hours.

One sultry afternoon, while the widow and her son were watching at his bedside, Takahama fell asleep. At the same moment a very large white butterfly entered the room, and perched upon the sick man's pillow. The nephew drove it away with a fan; but it returned immediately to the pillow, and was again driven away, only to come back a third time. Then the nephew chased it into the garden, and across the garden, through an open gate, into the cemetery of the neighbouring temple. But it continued to flutter before him as if unwilling to be driven further, and acted so queerly that he began to wonder whether it was really a butterfly, or a *ma*.[16] He again chased it, and followed it far into the cemetery, until he saw it fly against a tomb—a woman's tomb. There it unaccountably disappeared; and he searched for it in vain. He then examined the monument. It bore the personal name "Akiko", together with an unfamiliar family name, and an inscription stating that Akiko had died at the age of eighteen. Apparently the tomb had been erected about fifty years previously: moss had begun to gather upon it. But it had been well cared for: there were fresh flowers before it; and the water-tank had recently been filled.

On returning to the sick-room, the young man was shocked by the announcement that his uncle had ceased to breathe. Death had come to the sleeper painlessly; and the dead face smiled. The young man told his mother of what he had seen in the cemetery.

"Ah!" exclaimed the widow, "then it must have been Akiko!" . . .

"But who was Akiko, mother?" the nephew asked.

The widow answered:—

"When your good uncle was young, he was betrothed to a charming girl called Akiko, the daughter of a neighbour. Akiko died of consumption, only a little before the day appointed for the wedding; and her promised husband sorrowed greatly. After Akiko had been buried, he made a vow never to marry; and he built this little house beside the cemetery, so that he might be always near her grave. All this happened more than fifty years ago. And every day of those fifty years—winter and summer alike— your uncle went to the cemetery, and prayed at the grave, and swept the tomb, and set offerings before it. But he did not like to have any mention made of the matter; and he never spoke of it . . . So, at last, Akiko came for him: the white butterfly was her soul."

IV.

I had almost forgotten to mention an ancient Japanese dance, called the Butterfly Dance (*Kochō-Mai*), which used to be performed in the Imperial Palace, by dancers costumed as butterflies. Whether it is danced occasionally nowadays I do not know. It is said to be very difficult to learn. Six dancers are required for the proper performance of it; and they must move in particular figures—obeying traditional rules for every step, pose, or gesture—and circling about each other very slowly to the sound of handdrums and great drums, small flutes and great flutes, and pandean pipes of a form unknown to Western Pan.

Notes

[1] "The modest nymph beheld her God, and blushed." (Or, in a more familiar rendering: "The modest water saw its God, and blushed." In this line the double value of the word "*nympha*"—used by classical poets both in the meaning of fountain and in that of the divinity of a fountain, or spring—reminds one of that graceful playing with words which Japanese poets practice.

[2] More usually written "*nugi-kakéru*", which means either "to take off and hang up", or "to begin to take off"—as in the above poem. More loosely, but more effectively, the verses might thus be rendered: "Like a woman slipping off her *haori*—that is the appearance of a butterfly." One must have seen the Japanese garment described, to appreciate the comparison. The *haori* is a silk upper-dress—a kind of sleeved cloak—worn by both sexes; but the poem suggests a woman's *haori*, which is usually of richer colour or material. The sleeves are wide; and the lining is usually of brightly-coloured silk, often beautifully variegated. In taking off the *haori*, the brilliant lining is displayed—and at such an instant the fluttering splendour might well be likened to the appearance of a butterfly in motion.

[3] The bird-catcher's pole is smeared with bird-lime; and the verses suggest that the insect is preventing the man

Butterflies

from using his pole, by persistently getting in the way of it,—as the birds might take warning from seeing the butterfly limed. *Jama suru* means "to hinder" or "prevent".

[4] Even while it is resting, the wings of the butterfly may be seen to quiver at moments,—as if the creature were dreaming of flight.

[5] A little poem by Bashō, greatest of all Japanese composers of *hokku*. The verses are intended to suggest the joyous feeling of spring-time.

[6] Literally, "a windless day"; but two negatives in Japanese poetry do not necessarily imply an affirmative, as in English. The meaning is, that although there is no wind, the fluttering motion of the butterflies suggests, to the eyes at least, that a strong breeze is playing.

[7] Alluding to the Buddhist proverb: "*Rakkwa éda ni kaërazu; hakyō futatabi terasazu*" ("The fallen flower returns not to the branch; the broken mirror never again reflects"). So says the proverb—yet it seemed to me that I saw a fallen flower return to the branch . . . No: it was only a butterfly.

[8] Alluding probably to the light fluttering motion of falling cherry-petals.

[9] That is to say, the grace of their motion makes one think of the grace of young girls, daintily costumed, in robes with long fluttering sleeves . . . An old Japanese proverb declares that even a devil is pretty at eighteen: "*Oni mo jiu-hachi azami no hana*" ("Even a devil at eighteen, flower-of-the-thistle").

[10] Or perhaps the verses might be more effectively rendered thus: "Happy together, do you say? Yes—if we should be reborn as field-butterflies in some future life: then we might accord!" This poem was composed by the celebrated poet Issa, on the occasion of divorcing his wife.

[11] Or, "*Taré no tama?*"

[12] Literally, "Butterfly-pursuing heart I wish to have always"; that is, I would that I might always be able to find pleasure in simple things, like a happy child.

[13] An old popular error,—probably imported from China.

[14] A name suggested by the resemblance of the larva's artificial covering to the *mino*, or straw-raincoat, worn by Japanese peasants. I am not sure whether the dictionary rendering, "basket-worm", is quite correct;—but the larva commonly called *minomushi* does really construct for itself something much like the covering of the basket-worm.

[15] *Pyrus spectabilis.*

[16] An evil spirit.

蚊
Mosquitoes

With a view to self-protection I have been reading Doctor Howard's book, *Mosquitoes*. I am persecuted by mosquitoes. There are several species in my neighbourhood; but only one of them is a serious torment—a tiny needly thing, all silver-speckled and silver-streaked. The puncture of it is sharp as an electric burn; and the mere hum of it has a lancinating quality of tone which foretells the quality of the pain about to come—much in the same way that a particular smell suggests a particular taste. I find that this mosquito much resembles the creature which Doctor Howard calls *Stegomyia fasciata*, or *Culex fasciatus*: and that its habits are the same as those of the *Stegomyia*. For example, it is diurnal rather than nocturnal, and becomes most troublesome during the afternoon. And I have discovered that it comes from the Buddhist cemetery—a very old cemetery—in the rear of my garden.

Doctor Howard's book declares that, in order to rid a neighbourhood of mosquitoes, it is only necessary to pour a little petroleum, or kerosene oil, into the stagnant water where they breed. Once a week the oil should be used, "at the rate of one ounce for every fifteen square feet of water-surface, and a proportionate quantity for any less surface." . . . But please to consider the conditions in *my* neighbourhood!

I have said that my tormentors come from the Buddhist cemetery. Before nearly every tomb in that old cemetery there is a water-receptacle, or cistern, called "*mizutamé*". In the majority of cases this *mizutamé* is simply an oblong cavity chiselled in the broad pedestal supporting the monument; but before tombs of a costly kind, having no pedestal tank, a larger separate tank is placed, cut out of a single block of stone, and decorated with a family crest, or with symbolic carvings. In front of a tomb of the humblest class, having no *mizutamé*, water is placed in cups or other vessels—for the dead must have water. Flowers also must be offered to them; and before every tomb you will find a pair of bamboo cups, or other flower-vessels; and these, of course, contain water. There is a well in the cemetery to supply water for the graves. Whenever the tombs are visited by relatives and friends of the dead, fresh water is poured into the tanks and cups. But as an old cemetery of this kind contains thousands of *mizutamé*, and tens of thousands of flower-vessels, the water in all of these cannot be renewed every day. It becomes stagnant and populous. The deeper tanks seldom get dry;—the rainfall at Tōkyō being heavy enough to keep them partly filled during nine months out of the twelve.

Well, it is in these tanks and flower-vessels that mine enemies are born: they rise by millions from the water of the dead;—and, according to Buddhist doctrine, some of them may be reincarnations of those very dead, condemned by the error of former lives to the condition of *Jiki-ketsu-gaki*, or blood-drinking pretas . . . Anyhow the malevolence of the *Culex fasciatus* would justify the suspicion that some wicked human soul had been compressed into that wailing speck of a body . . .

Now, to return to the subject of kerosene oil, you can exterminate the mosquitoes of any locality by covering with a film of kerosene all stagnant water surfaces therein. The larvae die on rising to breathe; and the adult females perish when they approach the water to launch their rafts of eggs. And I read, in Doctor Howard's book, that the actual cost of freeing from mosquitoes one American town of fifty thousand inhabitants, does not exceed three hundred dollars! . . .

I wonder what would be said if the city government of Tōkyō—which is aggressively scientific and progressive—were suddenly to command that all water-surfaces in the Buddhist cemeteries should be covered, at regular intervals, with a film of kerosene oil! How could the religion which prohibits the taking of any life—even of invisible life—yield to such a mandate? Would filial piety even dream of consenting to obey such an order? And then to think of the cost, in labour and time, of putting kerosene oil, every seven days, into the millions of *mizutamé*, and the tens of millions of bamboo flower-cups, in the Tōkyō grave-yards! . . . Impossible! To free the city from mosquitoes it would be necessary to demolish the ancient graveyards;—and that would signify the ruin of the Buddhist temples attached to them;—and that would mean the disparition of so many charming gardens, with their lotus-ponds and Sanscrit-lettered monuments and humpy bridges and holy groves and weirdly-smiling Buddhas! So the extermination of the *Culex fasciatus* would involve the destruction of the poetry of the ancestral cult,—surely too great a price to pay! . . .

Besides, I should like, when my time comes, to be laid away in some Buddhist graveyard of the ancient kind— so that my ghostly company should be ancient, caring nothing for the fashions and the changes and the disintegrations of Meiji. That old cemetery behind my garden would be a suitable place. Everything there is beautiful with a beauty of exceeding and startling queerness; each tree and stone has been shaped by some old, old ideal which no longer exists in any living brain; even the shadows are not of this time and sun, but of a world forgotten, that never knew steam or electricity or magnetism or—kerosene oil! Also in the boom of the big bell there is a quaintness of tone which wakens feelings, so strangely far-away from all the nineteenth-century part of me, that the faint blind stirrings of them make me afraid,—deliciously afraid. Never do I hear that billowing peal but I become aware of a striving and a fluttering in the abyssal part of my ghost,—a sensation as of memories struggling to reach the light beyond the obscurations of a million million deaths and births. I hope to remain within hearing of that bell . . . And, considering the possibility of being doomed to the state of a *Jiki-ketsu-gaki*, I want to have my chance of being reborn in some bamboo flower-cup, or *mizutamé*, whence I might issue softly, singing my thin and pungent song, to bite some people that I know.

蟻
Ants

I.

This morning sky, after the night's tempest, is a pure and dazzling blue. The air—the delicious air!—is full of sweet resinous odours, shed from the countless pine-boughs broken and strewn by the gale. In the neighbouring bamboo-grove I hear the flute-call of the bird that praises the Sûtra of the Lotus; and the land is very still by reason of the south wind. Now the summer, long delayed, is truly with us: butterflies of queer Japanese colours are flickering about; sémi are wheezing; wasps are humming; gnats are dancing in the sun; and the ants are busy repairing their damaged habitations . . . I bethink me of a Japanese poem:

Yuku é naki:
   Ari no sumai ya!
      Go-getsu amé.

(Now the poor creature has nowhere to go! . . . Alas for the dwellings of the ants in this rain of the fifth month!)

But those big black ants in my garden do not seem to need any sympathy. They have weathered the storm in some unimaginable way, while great trees were being uprooted, and houses blown to fragments, and roads washed out of existence. Yet, before the typhoon, they took no other visible precaution than to block up the gates of their subterranean town. And the spectacle of their triumphant toil today impels me to attempt an essay on Ants.

I should have liked to preface my disquisitions with something from the old Japanese literature—something emotional or metaphysical. But all that my Japanese friends were able to find for me on the subject—excepting some verses of little worth—was Chinese. This Chinese material consisted chiefly of strange stories; and one of them seems to me worth quoting—*faute de mieux*.

છે

In the province of Taishū, in China, there was a pious man who, every day, during many years, fervently worshiped a certain goddess. One morning, while he was engaged in his devotions, a beautiful woman, wearing a yellow robe, came into his chamber and stood before him. He, greatly surprised, asked her what she wanted, and why she had entered unannounced. She answered: "I am not a woman: I am the goddess whom you have so long and so faithfully worshiped; and I have now come to prove to you that your devotion has not been in vain . . . Are you acquainted with the language of Ants?" The worshiper replied: "I am only a low-born and ignorant person—not a scholar; and even of the language of superior men I know nothing." At these words the goddess smiled, and drew from her bosom a little box, shaped like an incense box. She opened the box, dipped a finger into it, and took therefrom some kind of ointment with which she anointed the ears of the man. "Now," she said to him, "try to find some Ants, and when you find any, stoop down, and listen carefully to their talk. You will be able to understand it; and you will hear of something to your advantage . . . Only remember that you must not frighten or vex the Ants." Then the goddess vanished away.

The man immediately went out to look for some Ants. He had scarcely crossed the threshold of his door when he perceived two Ants upon a stone supporting one of the house-pillars. He stooped over them, and listened; and he was astonished to find that he could hear them talking, and could understand what they said. "Let us try to find a warmer place," proposed one of the Ants. "Why a warmer place?" asked the other;—"what is the matter with this place?" "It is too damp and cold below," said the first Ant; "there is a big treasure buried here; and the sunshine cannot warm the ground about it." Then the two Ants went away together, and the listener ran for a spade.

By digging in the neighbourhood of the pillar, he soon found a number of large jars full of gold coin. The discovery of this treasure made him a very rich man.

Afterwards he often tried to listen to the conversation of Ants. But he was never again able to hear them speak. The ointment of the goddess had opened his ears to their mysterious language for only a single day.

∞

Now I, like that Chinese devotee, must confess myself a very ignorant person, and naturally unable to hear the conversation of Ants. But the Fairy of Science sometimes touches my ears and eyes with her wand; and then, for a little time, I am able to hear things inaudible, and to perceive things imperceptible.

II.

For the same reason that it is considered wicked, in sundry circles, to speak of a non-Christian people having produced a civilisation ethically superior to our own, certain persons will not be pleased by what I am going to say about ants. But there are men, incomparably wiser than I can ever hope to be, who think about insects and civilisations independently of the blessings of Christianity; and I find encouragement in the new *Cambridge Natural History*, which contains the following remarks by Professor David Sharp, concerning ants:—

"Observation has revealed the most remarkable phenomena in the lives of these insects. Indeed we can scarcely avoid the conclusion that they have acquired, in many respects, the art of living together in societies more perfectly than our own species has; and that they have anticipated us in the acquisition of some of the industries and arts that greatly facilitate social life."

I suppose that few well-informed persons will dispute this plain statement by a trained specialist. The contemporary man of science is not apt to become sentimental about ants or bees; but he will not hesitate to acknowledge that, in regard to social evolution, these insects appear to have advanced "beyond man". Mr. Herbert Spencer, whom nobody will charge with romantic tendencies, goes considerably further than Professor Sharp; showing us that ants are, in a very real sense, *ethically* as well as economically in advance of humanity—their lives being entirely devoted to altruistic ends. Indeed, Professor Sharp somewhat needlessly qualifies his praise of the ant with this cautious observation:—

"The competence of the ant is not like that of man. It is devoted to the welfare of the species rather than to that of the individual, which is, as it were, sacrificed or specialised for the benefit of the community."

The obvious implication,—that any social state, in which the improvement of the individual is sacrificed to the common welfare, leaves much to be desired—is probably correct, from the actual human standpoint. For man is yet imperfectly evolved; and human society has much to gain from his further individuation. But in regard to social insects the implied criticism is open to question. "The improvement of the individual," says Herbert Spencer, "consists in the better fitting of him for social cooperation; and this, being conducive to social prosperity, is conducive to the maintenance of the race." In other words, the value of the individual can be *only* in relation to the society; and this granted, whether the sacrifice of the individual for the sake of that society be good or evil must depend upon what the society might gain or lose through a further individuation of its members . . . But, as we shall presently see, the conditions of ant-society that most deserve our attention are the ethical conditions; and these are beyond human criticism, since they realise that ideal of moral evolution described by Mr. Spencer as "a state in which egoism and altruism are so conciliated that the one merges into the other." That is to say, a state in which the only possible pleasure is the pleasure of unselfish action. Or, again to quote Mr. Spencer, the activities of the insect-society are "activities which postpone individual well-being so completely to the well-being of the community that individual life appears to be attended to only just so far as is necessary to make possible due attention to social life . . . the individual taking only just such food and just such rest as are needful to maintain its vigour."

III.

I hope my reader is aware that ants practice horticulture and agriculture; that they are skilful in the cultivation of mushrooms; that they have domesticated (according to present knowledge) five hundred and eighty-four different kinds of animals; that they make tunnels through solid rock; that they know how to provide against atmospheric changes which might endanger the health of their children; and that, for insects, their longevity is exceptional—members of the more highly evolved species living for a considerable number of years.

But it is not especially of these matters that I wish to speak. What I want to talk about is the awful propriety, the terrible morality, of the ant.[1] Our most appalling ideals of conduct fall short of the ethics of the ant—as progress is reckoned in time—by nothing less than millions of years! . . .When I say "the ant", I mean the highest type of ant—not, of course, the entire ant-family. About two thousand species of ants are already known; and these exhibit, in their social organisations, widely varying degrees of evolution. Certain social phenomena of the greatest biological importance, and of no less importance in their strange relation to the subject of ethics, can be studied to advantage only in the existence of the most highly evolved societies of ants.

After all that has been written of late years about the probable value of relative experience in the long life of the ant, I suppose that few persons would venture to deny individual character to the ant. The intelligence of the little creature in meeting and overcoming difficulties of a totally new kind, and in adapting itself to conditions entirely foreign to its experience, proves a considerable power of independent thinking. But this at least is certain: that the

Ants

ant has no individuality capable of being exercised in a purely selfish direction;—I am using the word "selfish" in its ordinary acceptation: a greedy ant, a sensual ant, an ant capable of any one of the seven deadly sins, or even of a small venial sin, is unimaginable. Equally unimaginable, of course, a romantic ant, an ideological ant, a poetical ant, or an ant inclined to metaphysical speculations. No human mind could attain to the absolute matter-of-fact quality of the ant-mind; no human being, as now constituted, could cultivate a mental habit so impeccably practical as that of the ant. But this superlatively practical mind is incapable of moral error. It would be difficult, perhaps, to prove that the ant has no religious ideas. But it is certain that such ideas could not be of any use to it. The being incapable of moral weakness is beyond the need of "spiritual guidance".

Only in a vague way can we conceive the character of ant-society, and the nature of ant-morality; and to do even this we must try to imagine some yet impossible state of human society and human morals. Let us, then, imagine a world full of people incessantly and furiously working—all of whom seem to be women. No one of these women could be persuaded or deluded into taking a single atom of food more than is needful to maintain her strength; and no one of them ever sleeps a second longer than is necessary to keep her nervous system in good working order. And all of them are so peculiarly constituted that the least unnecessary indulgence would result.

The work daily performed by these female labourers comprises road-making, bridge-building, timber-cutting, architectural construction of numberless kinds, horticulture and agriculture, the feeding and sheltering of a hundred varieties of domestic animals, the manufacture of sundry chemical products, the storage and conservation of countless food-stuffs, and the care of the children of the race. All this labour is done for the commonwealth—no citizen of which is capable even of thinking about "property", except as a *res publica*;—and the sole object of the commonwealth is the nurture and training of its young—nearly all of whom are girls. The period of infancy is long; the children remain for a great while, not only helpless, but shapeless, and withal so delicate that they must be very carefully guarded against the least change of temperature. Fortunately their nurses understand the laws of health: each thoroughly knows all that she ought to know in regard to ventilation, disinfection, drainage, moisture, and the danger of germs—germs being as visible, perhaps, to her myopic sight as they become to our own eyes under the microscope. Indeed, all matters of hygiene are so well comprehended that no nurse ever makes a mistake about the sanitary conditions of her neighbourhood.

In spite of this perpetual labour no worker remains unkempt: each is scrupulously neat, making her toilet many times a day. But as every worker is born with the most beautiful of combs and brushes attached to her wrists, no time is wasted in the toilet-room. Besides keeping themselves strictly clean, the workers must also keep their houses and gardens in faultless order, for the sake of the children. Nothing less than an earthquake, an eruption, an inundation, or a desperate war, is allowed to interrupt the daily routine of dusting, sweeping, scrubbing, and disinfecting.

IV.

Now for stranger facts:—

This world of incessant toil is a more than Vestal world. It is true that males can sometimes be perceived in it; but they appear only at particular seasons, and they have nothing whatever to do with the workers or with the work. None of them would presume to address a worker—except, perhaps, under extraordinary circumstances of common peril. And no worker would think of talking to a male;—for males, in this queer world, are inferior beings, equally incapable of fighting or working, and tolerated only as necessary evils. One special class of females,—the Mothers-Elect of the race,—do condescend to consort with males, during a very brief period, at particular seasons. But the Mothers-Elect do not work; and they *must* accept husbands. A worker could not even dream of keeping company with a male—not merely because such associations would signify the most frivolous waste of time, nor yet because the worker necessarily regards all males with unspeakable contempt; but because the worker is incapable of wedlock. Some workers, indeed, are capable of parthenogenesis, and give birth to children who never had fathers. As a general rule, however, the worker is truly feminine by her moral instincts only; she has all the tenderness, the patience, and the foresight that we call "maternal"; but her sex has disappeared, like the sex of the Dragon-Maiden in the Buddhist legend.

For defence against creatures of prey, or enemies of the state, the workers are provided with weapons; and they are furthermore protected by a large military force. The warriors are so much bigger than the workers (in some communities, at least) that it is difficult, at first sight, to believe them of the same race. Soldiers one hundred times larger than the workers whom they guard are not uncommon. But all these soldiers are Amazons,—or, more correctly speaking, sémi-females. They can work sturdily; but being built for fighting and for heavy pulling chiefly, their usefulness is restricted to those directions in which force, rather than skill, is required.

(Why females, rather than males, should have been evolutionally specialised into soldiery and labourers may not be nearly so simple a question as it appears. I am very sure of not being able to answer it. But natural economy may have decided the matter. In many forms of life, the female greatly exceeds the male in bulk and in energy;—perhaps, in this case, the larger reserve of life-force possessed originally by the complete female could be more rapidly and effectively utilised for the development of a special fighting-caste. All energies which, in the fertile female, would be expended in the giving of life seem here to have been diverted to the evolution of aggressive power, or working-capacity.)

Of the true females—the Mothers-Elect—there are very few indeed; and these are treated like queens. So constantly and so reverentially are they waited upon that they can seldom have any wishes to express. They are relieved from every care of existence,—except the duty of bearing offspring. Night and day they are cared for in every possible manner. They alone are superabundantly and richly fed:—for the sake of the offspring they must eat and drink and repose right royally; and their physiological specialisation allows of such indulgence *ad libitum*. They seldom go out, and never unless attended by a powerful escort; as they cannot be permitted to incur unnecessary fatigue or danger. Probably they have no great desire to go out. Around them revolves the whole activity of the race: all its intelligence and toil and thrift are directed solely toward the well-being of these Mothers and of their children.

But last and least of the race rank the husbands of these Mothers,—the necessary Evils,—the males. They appear only at a particular season, as I have already observed; and their lives are very short. Some cannot even boast of noble descent, though destined to royal wedlock; for they are not royal offspring, but virgin-born,—parthenogenetic children,—and, for that reason especially, inferior beings, the chance results of some mysterious atavism. But of any sort of males the commonwealth tolerates but few,—barely enough to serve as husbands for the Mothers-Elect, and these few perish almost as soon as their duty has been done. The meaning of Nature's law, in this extraordinary world, is identical with Ruskin's teaching that life without effort is crime; and since the males are useless as workers or fighters their existence is of only momentary importance. They are not, indeed, sacrificed,—like the Aztec victim chosen for the festival of Tezcatlipoca, and allowed a honeymoon of twenty days before his heart was torn out. But they are scarcely less unfortunate in their high fortune. Imagine youths brought up in the knowledge that they are destined to become royal bridegrooms for a single night,—that after their bridal they will have no moral right to live,—that marriage, for each and all of them, will signify certain death,—and that they cannot even hope to be lamented by their young widows, who will survive them for a time of many generations . . . !

V.

But all the foregoing is no more than a proem to the real "Romance of the Insect-World".

By far the most startling discovery in relation to this astonishing civilisation is that of the suppression of sex. In certain advanced forms of ant-life sex totally disappears in the majority of individuals;—in nearly all the higher ant-societies sex-life appears to exist only to the extent absolutely needed for the continuance of the species. But the biological fact in itself is much less startling than the ethical suggestion which it offers;—*for this practical sup-*

pression, or regulation, of sex-faculty appears to be voluntary! Voluntary, at least, so far as the species is concerned. It is now believed that these wonderful creatures have learned how to develop, or to arrest the development, of sex in their young,—by some particular mode of nutrition. They have succeeded in placing under perfect control what is commonly supposed to be the most powerful and unmanageable of instincts. And this rigid restraint of sex-life to within the limits necessary to provide against extinction is but one (though the most amazing) of many vital economies effected by the race. Every capacity for egoistic pleasure—in the common meaning of the word "egoistic"—has been equally repressed through physiological modification. No indulgence of any natural appetite is possible except to that degree in which such indulgence can directly or indirectly benefit the species;—even the indispensable requirements of food and sleep being satisfied only to the exact extent necessary for the maintenance of healthy activity. The individual can exist, act, think, only for the communal good; and the commune triumphantly refuses, in so far as cosmic law permits, to let itself be ruled either by Love or Hunger.

Most of us have been brought up in the belief that without some kind of religious creed—some hope of future reward or fear of future punishment—no civilisation could exist. We have been taught to think that in the absence of laws based upon moral ideas, and in the absence of an effective police to enforce such laws, nearly everybody would seek only his or her personal advantage, to the disadvantage of everybody else. The strong would then destroy the weak; pity and sympathy would disappear; and the whole social fabric would fall to pieces . . . These teachings confess the existing imperfection of human nature; and they contain obvious truth. But those who first proclaimed that truth, thousands and thousands of years ago, never imagined a form of social existence in which selfishness would be *naturally* impossible. It remained for irreligious Nature to furnish us with proof positive that there can exist a society in which the pleasure of active beneficence makes needless the idea of duty,—a society in which instinctive morality can dispense with ethical codes of every sort,—a society of which every member is born so absolutely unselfish, and so energetically good, that moral training could signify, even for its youngest, neither more nor less than waste of precious time.

To the Evolutionist such facts necessarily suggest that the value of our moral idealism is but temporary; and that something better than virtue, better than kindness, better than self-denial,—in the present human meaning of those terms,—might, under certain conditions, eventually replace them. He finds himself obliged to face the question whether a world without moral notions might not be morally better than a world in which conduct is regulated by such notions. He must even ask himself whether the existence of religious commandments, moral laws, and ethical standards among ourselves does not prove us still in a very primitive stage of social evolution. And these questions naturally lead up to another: Will humanity ever be able, on this planet, to reach an ethical condition beyond all its ideals,—a condition in which everything that we now call evil will have been atrophied out of existence, and everything that we call virtue have been transmuted into instinct;—a state of altruism in which ethical concepts and codes will have become as useless as they would be, even now, in the societies of the higher ants.

The giants of modern thought have given some attention to this question; and the greatest among them has answered it,—partly in the affirmative. Herbert Spencer has expressed his belief that humanity will arrive at some state of civilisation ethically comparable with that of the ant:—

"If we have, in lower orders of creatures, cases in which the nature is constitutionally so modified that altruistic activities have become one with egoistic activities, there is an irresistible implication that a parallel identification will, under parallel conditions, take place among human beings. Social insects furnish us with instances completely to the point,—and instances showing us, indeed, to what a marvellous degree the life of the individual may be absorbed in subserving the lives of other individuals . . . Neither the ant nor the bee can be supposed to have a sense of duty, in the acceptation we give to that word; nor can it be supposed that it is continually undergoing self-sacrifice, in the ordinary acceptation of that word . . . [The facts] show us that it is within the possibilities of organisation to produce a nature which shall be just as energetic and even more energetic in the pursuit of altruistic ends, as is, in other cases, shown in the pursuit of egoistic ends;—and they show that, in such cases, these altruistic ends are pursued in pursuing ends which, on their other face, are egoistic. For the satisfaction of the needs of the organisation, these actions, conducive to the welfare of others, *must* be carried on . . . "

ಞ

So far from its being true that there must go on, throughout all the future, a condition in which self-regard is to be continually subjected by the regard for others, it will, contrari-wise, be the case that a regard for others will eventually become so large a source of pleasure as to overgrow the pleasure which is derivable from direct egoistic gratification . . . Eventually, then, there will come also a state in which egoism and altruism are so conciliated that the one merges in the other.

VI.

Of course the foregoing prediction does not imply that human nature will ever undergo such physiological change as would be represented by structural specialisations comparable to those by which the various castes of insect-societies are differentiated. We are not bidden to imagine a future state of humanity in which the active majority would consist of sémi-female workers and Amazons toiling for an inactive minority of selected Mothers. Even in his chapter, "Human Population in the Future", Mr. Spencer has attempted no detailed statement of the physical modifications inevitable to the production of higher moral types,—though his general statement in regard to a perfected nervous system, and a great diminution of human fertility, suggests that such moral evolution would signify a very considerable amount of physical change. If it be legitimate to believe in a future humanity to which the pleasure of mutual beneficence will represent the whole joy of life, would it not also be legitimate to imagine other transformations, physical and moral, which the facts of insect-biology have proved to be within the range of evolutional possibility? . . . I do not know. I most worshipfully reverence Herbert Spencer as the greatest philosopher that has yet appeared in this world; and I should be very sorry to write down anything contrary to his teaching, in such wise that the reader could imagine it to have been inspired by the Synthetic Philosophy. For the ensuing reflections, I alone am responsible; and if I err, let the sin be upon my own head.

I suppose that the moral transformations predicted by Mr. Spencer could be effected only with the aid of physiological change, and at a terrible cost. Those ethical conditions manifested by insect societies can have been reached only through effort desperately sustained for millions of years against the most atrocious necessities. Necessities equally merciless may have to be met and mastered eventually by the human race. Mr. Spencer has shown that the time of the greatest possible human suffering is yet to come, and that it will be concomitant with the period of the greatest possible pressure of population. Among other results of that long stress, I understand that there will be a vast increase of human intelligence and sympathy: and that this increase of intelligence will be effected at the cost of human fertility. But this decline in reproductive power will not, we are told, be sufficient to assure the very highest social conditions: it will only relieve that pressure of population which has been the main cause of human suffering. The state of perfect social equilibrium will be approached, but never quite reached, by mankind:—

> *Unless there be discovered some means of solving economic problems, just as social insects have solved them, by the suppression of sex-life.*

Supposing that such a discovery were made, and that the human race should decide to arrest the development of sex in the majority of its young,—so as to effect a transference of those forces, now demanded by sex-life to the development of higher activities,—might not the result be an eventual state of polymorphism, like that of ants? And, in such event, might not the Coming Race be indeed represented in its higher types,—through feminine rather than masculine evolution,—by a majority of beings of neither sex?

Considering how many persons, even now, through merely unselfish (not to speak of religious) motives, sentence themselves to celibacy, it should not appear improbable that a more highly evolved humanity would cheerfully sacrifice a large proportion of its sex-life for the common weal, particularly in view of certain advantages to be gained. Not the least of such advantages,—always supposing that mankind were able to control sex-life after the natural manner of the ants,—would be a prodigious increase of longevity. The higher types of a humanity superior to sex might be able to realise the dream of life for a thousand years.

Already we find our lives too short for the work we have to do; and with the constantly accelerating progress of discovery, and the never-ceasing expansion of knowledge, we shall certainly find more and more reason to regret, as time goes on, the brevity of existence. That Science will ever discover the Elixir of the Alchemists' hope is extremely unlikely. The Cosmic Powers will not allow us to cheat them. For every advantage which they yield us the full price must be paid: nothing for nothing is the everlasting law. Perhaps the price of long life will prove to be the price that the ants have paid for it. Perhaps, upon some elder planet, that price has already been paid, and the power to produce offspring restricted to a caste morphologically differentiated, in unimaginable ways, from the rest of the species . . .

VII.

But while the facts of insect-biology suggest so much in regard to the future course of human evolution, do they not also suggest something of largest significance concerning the relation of ethics to cosmic law? Apparently, the highest evolution will not be permitted to creatures capable of what human moral experience has in all eras condemned. Apparently, the highest possible strength is the strength of unselfishness; and power supreme never will be accorded to cruelty or to lust. There may be no gods; but the forces that shape and dissolve all forms of being would seem to be much more exacting than gods. To prove a "dramatic tendency" in the ways of the stars is not possible; but the cosmic process seems nevertheless to affirm the worth of every human system of ethics fundamentally opposed to human egoism.

Note

[1] An interesting fact in this connection is that the Japanese word for ant, "*ari*", is represented by an ideograph formed of the character for "insect" combined with the character signifying "moral rectitude", "propriety" (*giri*). So the Chinese character actually means "The Propriety-Insect".

蠅物語
Story of a Fly

About two hundred years ago, there lived in Kyōto a merchant named Kazariya Kyūbei. His shop was in the street called Teramachidōri, a little south of the Shimabara thoroughfare. He had a maidservant named Tama,—a native of the province of Wakasa.

Tama was kindly treated by Kyūbei and his wife, and appeared to be sincerely attached to them. But she never cared to dress nicely, like other girls; and whenever she had a holiday she would go out in her working-dress, notwithstanding that she had been given several pretty robes. After she had been in the service of Kyūbei for about five years, he one day asked her why she never took any pains to look neat.

Tama blushed at the reproach implied by this question, and answered respectfully:—

"When my parents died, I was a very little girl; and, as they had no other child, it became my duty to have the Buddhist services performed on their behalf. At that time I could not obtain the means to do so; but I resolved to have their *ihai* (mortuary tablets) placed in the temple called Jōrakuji, and to have the rites performed, so soon as I could earn the money required. And in order to fulfill this resolve I have tried to be saving of my money and my clothes;— perhaps I have been too saving, as you have found me negligent of my person. But I have already been

Story of a Fly

able to put by about one hundred *mommé* of silver for the purpose which I have mentioned; and hereafter I will try to appear before you looking neat. So I beg that you will kindly excuse my past negligence and rudeness."

Kyūbei was touched by this simple confession; and he spoke to the girl kindly,—assuring her that she might consider herself at liberty thenceforth to dress as she pleased, and commending her filial piety.

Soon after this conversation, the maid Tama was able to have the tablets of her parents placed in the temple Jōrakuji, and to have the appropriate services performed. Of the money which she had saved she thus expended seventy *mommé*; and the remaining thirty *mommé* she asked her mistress to keep for her.

But early in the following winter Tama was suddenly taken ill; and after a brief sickness she died, on the eleventh day of the first month of the fifteenth year of Genroku (1702). Kyūbei and his wife were much grieved by her death.

Now, about ten days later, a very large fly came in to the house, and began to fly round and round the head of Kyūbei. This surprised Kyūbei, because no flies of any kind appear, as a rule, during the Period of Greatest Cold, and the larger kinds of flies are seldom seen except in the warm season. The fly annoyed Kyūbei so persistently that he took the trouble to catch it, and put it out of the house being careful the while to injure it in no way; for he was a devout Buddhist. It soon came back again; and was again caught and thrown out; but it entered a third time. Kyūbei's wife thought this a strange thing. "I wonder," she said, "if it is Tama." (For the dead,—particularly those who pass to the state of *Gaki*,—sometimes return in the form of insects.) Kyūbei laughed, and made answer, "Perhaps we can find out by marking it." He caught the fly, and slightly nicked the tips of its wings with a pair of scissors,—after which he carried it to a considerable distance from the house and let it go.

Next day it returned. Kyūbei still doubted whether its return had any ghostly significance. He caught it again, painted its wings and body with *beni* (rouge), carried it away from the house to a much greater distance than before, and set it free. But, two days later, it came back, all red; and Kyūbei ceased to doubt.

"I think it is Tama," he said. "She wants something;—but what does she want?"

The wife responded:—

"I have still thirty *mommé* of her savings. Perhaps she wants us to pay that money to the temple, for a Buddhist service on behalf of her spirit. Tama was always very anxious about her next birth."

As she spoke, the fly fell from the paper window on which it had been resting. Kyūbei picked it up, and found that it was dead.

Thereupon the husband and wife resolved to go to the temple at once, and to pay the girl's money to the priests. They put the body of the fly into a little box, and took it along with them. Jiku Shōnin, the chief priest of the temple, on hearing the story of the fly, decided that Kyūbei and his wife had acted rightly in the matter. Then Jiku Shōnin performed a *Ségaki* service on behalf of the spirit of Tama; and over the body of the fly were recited the eight rolls of the *sūtra Myōten*. And the box containing the body of the fly was buried in the grounds of the temple; and above the place a *sotoba* was set up, appropriately inscribed.

螢
Fireflies

I.

I want to talk about Japanese fireflies, but not entomologically. If you are interested, as you ought to be, in the scientific side of the subject, you should seek enlightenment from a Japanese professor of biology, now lecturing at the Imperial University of Tōkyō. He signs himself "Mr. S. Watasé" (the "S" standing for the personal name Shozaburo); and he has been a teacher as well as a student of science in America, where a number of his lectures have been published,[1]—lectures upon animal phosphorescence, animal electricity, the light producing organs of insects and fishes, and other wonderful topics of biology. He can tell you all that is known concerning the morphology of fireflies, the physiology of fireflies, the photometry of fireflies, the chemistry of their luminous substance, the spectroscopic analysis of their light, and the significance of that light in terms of ether-vibration. By experiment he can show you that, under normal conditions of temperature and environment, the number of light-pulsations produced by one species of Japanese firefly averages twenty-six per minute; and that the rate suddenly rises to sixty-three per minute, if the insect be frightened by seizure. Also he can prove to you that another and smaller kind of firefly, when taken in the hand, will increase the

number of its light-pulsings to upward of two hundred per minute. He suggests that the light may be of some protective value to the insect,—like the "warning colours" of sundry nauseous caterpillars and butterflies,—because the firefly has a very bitter taste, and birds appear to find it unpalatable. (Frogs, he has observed, do not mind the bad taste: they fill their cold bellies with fireflies till the light shines through them, much as the light of a candle-flame will glow through a porcelain jar.) But whether of protective value or not, the tiny dynamo would seem to be used in a variety of ways,—as a photo-telegraph, for example. As other insects converse by sound or by touch, the firefly utters its emotion in luminous pulsings: its speech is a language of light . . . I am only giving you some hints about the character of the professor's lectures, which are never merely technical. And for the best part of this non-scientific essay of mine,—especially that concerning the capture and the sale of fireflies in Japan,—I am indebted to some delightful lectures which he delivered last year to Japanese audiences in Tōkyō.

II.

As written to-day, the Japanese name of the firefly (*hotaru*) is ideographically composed with the sign for fire, doubled, above the sign for insect. The real origin of the word is nevertheless doubtful; and various etymologies have been suggested. Some scholars think that the appellation anciently signified "the First-born of Fire"; while others believe that it was first composed with syllables meaning "star" and "drop". The more poetical of the proposed derivations, I am sorry to say, are considered the least probable. But whatever may have been the primal meaning of the word *hotaru*, there can be no doubt as to

Insect Literature

the romantic quality of certain folk-names still given to the insect.

Two species of firefly have a wide distribution in Japan; and these have been popularly named *Genji-hotaru* and *Heiké-hotaru*: that is to say, "the Minamoto-Firefly" and "the Taira-Firefly." A legend avers that these fireflies are the ghosts of the old Minamoto and Taira warriors; that, even in their insect shapes, they remember the awful clan-struggle of the twelfth century; and that once every year, on the night of the twentieth day of the fourth month,[2] they fight a great battle on the Uji River. Therefore, on that night all caged fireflies should be set free, in order that they may be able to take part in the contest.

The *Genji-hotaru* is the largest of Japanese fireflies,— the largest species, at least, in Japan proper, not including the Loochoo Islands. It is found in almost every part of the country from Kyūshū to Ōshū. The *Heiké-hotaru* ranges farther north, being especially common in Yezo; but it is found also in the central and southern provinces. It is smaller than the Genji, and emits a feebler light. The fireflies commonly sold, by insect-dealers in Tōkyō, Ōsaka, Kyōto, and other cities, are of the larger species. Japanese observers have described the light of both insects as "tea-coloured" (*cha-iro*),—the tint of the ordinary Japanese infusion, when the leaf is of good quality, being a clear greenish yellow. But the light of a fine Genji-firefly is so brilliant that only a keen eye can detect the greenish color: at first sight the flash appears yellow as the flame of a wood-fire, and its vivid brightness has not been overpraised in the following *hokku*:—

Kagaribi mo
  Hotaru mo hikaru—
    Genji kana!

(Whether it be a glimmering of festal-fires[3] [far away], or a glimmering of fireflies [one can hardly tell]—ah, it is the Genji!)

Although the appellations *Genji-hotaru* and *Heiké-hotaru* are still in general use, both insects are known by other folk-names. In different provinces the Genji is called *Ō-hotaru*, or "Great Firefly"; *Ushi-hotaru*, or "Ox Firefly"; *Kuma-hotaru*, or "Bear Firefly"; and *Uji-hotaru*, or "Firefly of Uji",—not to mention such picturesque appellations as *Komosō-hotaru* and *Yamabuki-hotaru*, which could not be appreciated by the average Western reader. The *Heiké-hotaru* is also called *Hime-hotaru*, or "Princess Firefly"; *Nennéi-hotaru*, or "Baby Firefly"; and *Yuréi-hotaru*, or "Ghost Firefly". But these are only examples chosen at random: in almost every part of Japan there is a special folk name for the insect.

III.

There are many places in Japan which are famous for fireflies,—places which people visit in summer merely to enjoy the sight of the fireflies. Anciently the most celebrated of all such places was a little valley near Ishiyama, by the lake of Ōmi. It is still called Hotaru-Dani, or the Valley of Fireflies. Before the Period of Genroku (1688-1703), the swarming of the fireflies in this valley, during the sultry season, was accounted one of the natural marvels of the country. The fireflies of the Hotaru-Dani are still celebrated for their size; but that wonderful swarming of them, which old writers described, is no longer to be seen there. At present the most famous place for fireflies is in the neighbourhood of Uji, in Yamashiro. Uji, a pretty little town in the centre of the celebrated tea-district, is situated on the Ujigawa, and is scarcely less famed for its fireflies than for its teas. Every summer special trains run from Kyōto and Ōsaka to Uji, bringing thousands of visitors to see the fireflies. But it is on the river, at a point several miles from the town, that the great spectacle is to be witnessed,—the *Hotaru-Kassen*, or Firefly Battle. The stream there winds between hills covered with vegetation; and myriads of fireflies dart from either bank, to meet and cling above the water. At moments they so swarm together as to form what appears to the eye like a luminous cloud, or like a great ball of sparks. The cloud soon scatters, or the ball drops and breaks upon the surface of the current, and the fallen fireflies drift glittering away; but another swarm quickly collects in the same locality. People wait all night in boats upon the river to watch the phenomenon. After the *Hotaru-Kassen* is done, the Ujikawa, covered with the still sparkling bodies of the drifting insects, is said to appear like the Milky Way, or, as the Japanese more poetically call it, the River of Heaven.

Perhaps it was after witnessing such a spectacle that the great female poet, Chiyo of Kaga, composed these verses:—

Kawa bakari,
Yami wa nagarété—?
Hotaru kana!

(Which may be thus freely rendered: Is it the river only?—or is the darkness itself drifting? . . . Oh, the fireflies! . . . [4])

IV.

Many persons in Japan earn their living during the summer months by catching and selling fireflies: indeed, the

Fireflies

extent of this business entitles it to be regarded as a special industry. The chief centre of this industry is the region about Ishiyama, in Goshū, by the Lake of Ōmi,—a number of houses there supplying fireflies to many parts of the country, and especially to the great cities of Ōsaka and Kyōto. From sixty to seventy firefly-catchers are employed by each of the principal houses during the busy season. Some training is required for the occupation. A tyro might find it no easy matter to catch a hundred fireflies in a single night; but an expert has been known to catch three thousand. The methods of capture, although of the simplest possible kind, are very interesting to see.

Immediately after sunset, the firefly-hunter goes forth, with a long bamboo pole upon his shoulder, and a long bag of brown mosquito-netting wound, like a girdle, about his waist. When he reaches a wooded place frequented by fireflies,—usually some spot where willows are planted, on the bank of a river or lake,—he halts and watches the trees. As soon as the trees begin to twinkle satisfactorily, he gets his net ready, approaches the most luminous tree, and with his long pole strikes the branches. The fireflies, dislodged by the shock, do not immediately take flight, as more active insects would do under like circumstances, but drop helplessly to the ground, beetle-wise, where their light,—always more brilliant in moments of fear or pain,—renders them conspicuous. If suffered to remain upon the ground for a few moments, they will fly away. But the catcher, picking them up with astonishing quickness, using both hands at once, deftly tosses them *into his mouth*,—because he cannot lose the time required to put them, one by one, into the bag. Only when his mouth can hold no more, does he drop the fireflies, unharmed, into the netting.

Thus the firefly-catcher works until about two o'clock in the morning,—the old Japanese hour of ghosts,—at which time the insects begin to leave the trees and seek the dewy soil. There they are said to bury their tails, so as to remain viewless. But now the hunter changes his tactics. Taking a bamboo broom he brushes the surface of the turf, lightly and quickly. Whenever touched or alarmed by the broom, the fireflies display their lanterns, and are immediately nipped and bagged. A little before dawn, the hunters return to town.

At the firefly-shops the captured insects are sorted as soon as possible, according to the brilliancy of their light,—the more luminous being the higher-priced. Then they are put into gauze-covered boxes or cages, with a certain quantity of moistened grass in each cage. From one hundred to two hundred fireflies are placed in a single cage, according to grade. To these cages are attached small wooden tablets inscribed with the names of customers,— such as hotel proprietors, restaurant-keepers, wholesale and retail insect-merchants, and private persons who have ordered large quantities of fireflies for some particular festivity. The boxes are dispatched to their destinations by nimble messengers,—for goods of this class cannot be safely entrusted to express companies.

Great numbers of fireflies are ordered for display at evening parties in the summer season. A large Japanese guestroom usually overlooks a garden; and during a banquet or other evening entertainment, given in the sultry season, it is customary to set fireflies at liberty in the garden after sunset, that the visitors may enjoy the sight of the sparkling. Restaurant-keepers purchase largely. In the famous Dōtombori of Ōsaka, there is a house where myriads of fireflies are kept in a large space enclosed by mosquito-netting; and customers of this house are permitted to enter the enclosure and capture a certain number of fireflies to take home with them.

Fireflies

The wholesale price of living fireflies ranges from three *sen* per hundred up to thirteen *sen* per hundred, according to season and quality. Retail dealers sell them in cages; and in Tōkyō the price of a cage of fireflies ranges from three *sen* up to several dollars. The cheapest kind of cage, containing only three or four fireflies, is scarcely more than two inches square; but the costly cages,—veritable marvels of bamboo work, beautifully decorated,—are as large as cages for song-birds. Firefly cages of charming or fantastic shapes,—model houses, junks, temple-lanterns, etc.,—can be bought at prices ranging from thirty *sen* up to one dollar.

Dead or alive, fireflies are worth money. They are delicate insects, and they live but a short time in confinement. Great numbers die in the insect shops; and one celebrated insect-house is said to dispose every season of no less than five *sho*— that is to say, about one peck—of dead fireflies, which are sold to manufacturing establishments in Ōsaka. Formerly fireflies were used much more than at present in the manufacture of poultices and pills, and in the preparation of drugs peculiar to the practice of Chinese medicine. Even to-day some curious extracts are obtained from them; and one of these, called *Hotaru-no-abura*, or "firefly grease", is still used by woodworkers for the purpose of imparting rigidity to objects made of bent bamboo.

A very curious chapter on firefly-medicine might be written by somebody learned in the old-fashioned literature. The queerest part of the subject is Chinese, and belongs much more to demonology than to therapeutics. Firefly-ointments used to be made which had power, it was alleged, to preserve a house from the attacks of robbers, to counteract the effect of any poison, and to drive away "the hundred devils". And pills were made with firefly-substance which were believed to confer invulnerability;—one kind of such pills being called *Kanshōgan*, or "Commander-in-Chief Pills"; and another, *Buigan*, or "Military-Power Pills".

V.

Fire-fly-catching, as a business, is comparatively modern; but firefly-hunting, as a diversion, is a very old custom. Anciently it was an aristocratic amusement; and great nobles used to give firefly-hunting parties,—*hotaru-gari*. In this busy era of Meiji the *hotaru-gari* is rather an amusement for children than for grown-up folks; but the latter occasionally find time to join in the sport. All over Japan, the children have their firefly-hunts every summer;—moonless nights being usually chosen for such expeditions. Girls follow the chase with paper fans; boys, with long light poles, to the ends of which wisps of fresh bamboo-grass are tied. When struck down by a fan or a wisp, the insects are easily secured, as they are slow to take wing after having once been checked in actual flight. While hunting, the children sing little songs, supposed to attract the shining prey. These songs differ according to locality; and the number of them is wonderful. But there are very few possessing that sort of interest which justifies quotation. Two examples will probably suffice:

(Province of Chōshū)
Hotaru, koi! koi!
Koi-tomosé!
Nippon ichi no
Josan ga,
Chōchin tomoshité,
Koi to ina!

Fireflies

(Come, firefly, come! Come with your light burning! The nicest girl in Japan wants to know if you will not light your lantern and come!)

(Dialect of Shimonoséki)
Hochin, koi!
Hochin, koi!
Séki no machi no bon-san ga,
Chōchin tomoshité,
Koi!
Koi!

(Fire-fly, come! fire-fly, come! All the boys of Séki [want you to come] with your lantern lighted! Come! come!)

Of course, in order to hunt fireflies successfully, it is necessary to know something about their habits; and on this subject Japanese children are probably better informed than a majority of my readers, for whom the following notes may possess a novel interest:—

Fireflies frequent the neighbourhood of water, and like to circle above it; but some kinds are repelled by impure or stagnant water, and are only to be found in the vicinity of clear streams or lakes. The Genji-firefly shuns swamps, ditches, or foul canals; while the Heiké-firefly seems to be satisfied with any water. All fireflies seek by preference grassy banks shaded by trees; but they dislike certain trees and are attracted by others. They avoid pine trees, for instance; and they will not light upon rose-bushes. But upon willow-trees,—especially weeping willows,—they gather in great swarms. Occasionally, on a summer night, you may see a drooping willow so covered and illuminated with fireflies that all its branches appear "to be budding fire". During a bright moonlight night fireflies keep as much as possible in shadow; but when pursued they fly at once into the moonshine, where their shimmering is less easily perceived. Lamplight, or any strong artificial light, drives them away; but small bright lights attract them. They can be lured, for example, by the sparkling of a small piece of lighted charcoal, or by the glow of a little Japanese pipe, kindled in the dark. But the lamping of a single lively firefly, confined in a bottle, or cup, of clear glass, is the best of all lures.

As a rule the children hunt only in parties, for obvious reasons. In former years it would have been deemed foolhardy to go alone in pursuit of fireflies, because there existed certain uncanny beliefs concerning them. And in some of the country districts these beliefs still prevail. What appear to be fireflies may be malevolent spirits, or goblin-fires, or fox-lights, kindled to delude the wayfarer. Even real fireflies are not always to be trusted;—the weirdness of their kinships might be inferred from their love of willow-trees. Other trees have their particular spirits, good or evil, hamadryads or goblins; but the willow is particularly the tree of the dead,—the favourite of human ghosts. Any firefly may be a ghost,—who can tell? Besides, there is an old belief that the soul of a person still alive may sometimes assume the shape of a firefly. And here is a little story that was told me in Izuno:—

One cold winter's night a young *shizoku* of Matsuē, while on his way home from a wedding-party, was surprised to perceive a firefly-light hovering above the canal in front of his dwelling. Wondering that such an insect should be flying abroad in the season of snow, he stopped to look at it; and the light suddenly shot toward him. He struck at it with a stick; but it darted away, and flew into the garden of a residence adjoining his own.

Fireflies

Next morning he made a visit to that house, intending to relate the adventure to his neighbours and friends. But before he found a chance to speak of it, the eldest daughter of the family, happening to enter the guest-room without knowing of the young man's visit, uttered a cry of surprise, and exclaimed, "Oh! how you startled me! No one told me that you had called; and just as I came in I was thinking about you. Last night I had so strange a dream! I was flying in my dream,—flying above the canal in front of our house. It seemed very pleasant to fly over the water; and while I was flying there I saw you coming along the bank. Then I went to you to tell you that I had learned how to fly; but you struck at me, and frightened me so that I still feel afraid when I think of it . . . " After hearing this, the visitor thought it best not to relate his own experience for the time being, lest the coincidence should alarm the girl, to whom he was betrothed.

VI.

Fireflies have been celebrated in Japanese poetry from ancient time; and frequent mention of them is made in early classical prose. One of the fifty-four chapters of the famous novel, *Genji-Monogari*, for example,—written either toward the close of the tenth century or at the beginning of the eleventh,—is entitled, "Fireflies"; and the author relates how a certain noble person was enabled to obtain one glimpse of a lady's face in the dark by the device of catching and suddenly liberating a number of fireflies. The first literary interest in fireflies may have been stimulated, if not aroused, by the study of Chinese poetry. Even to-day every Japanese child knows a little song about the famous Chinese scholar who, in the time of his struggles with poverty, studied by the light of a paper bag filled with fireflies. But, whatever the original source of their inspiration, Japanese poets have been making verses about fireflies during more than a thousand years. Compositions on the subject can be found in every form of Japanese poetry; but the greater number of firefly poems are in *hokku*,—the briefest of all measures, consisting of only seventeen syllables. Modern love-poems relating to the firefly are legion; but the majority of these, written in the popular twenty-six-syllable form called *dodoītsu* appear to consist of little more than variants of one old classic fancy, comparing the silent burning of the insect's light to the consuming passion that is never uttered.

Perhaps my readers will be interested by the following selection of firefly poems. Some of the compositions are many centuries old:

"Catching Fireflies"

Mayoi-go no
  Naku-naku tsukamu
    Hotaru kana!

(Ah! the lost child! Though crying and crying, still he catches fireflies!)

Kuraki yori
  Kuraki hito yobu:
    Hotaru kana!

(Out of the blackness black people call [to each other]: [they are hunting] fireflies!)

Iu koto no
  Kikoēté ya, takaku
    Tobu hotaru!

Fireflies

(Ah! having heard the voices of people [crying "Catch it!"], the firefly now flies higher!)

Owarété wa
  Tsuki ni kakururu
    Hotaru kana!

(Ah, [the cunning] fireflies! being chased, they hide themselves in the moonlight!)

Ubayoté
  Fumi-koroshitaru
    Hotaru kana!

([Two firefly-catchers] having tried to seize it [at the same time], the poor firefly is trampled to death!)

"The Light of Fireflies"

Hotarubi ya!
  Mada kuréyaranu,
    Hashi no uri.

(Fireflies already sparkling under the bridge,—and it is not yet dark!)

Mizu-gusa no
  Kururu to miété
    Tobu hotaru.

(When the water-grasses appear to grow dark, the fireflies begin to fly.[5])

Oku-no-ma yé
  Hanashité mitaru
    Hotaru kana!

(Pleasant, from the guest-room,[6] to watch the fire-flies being set free in the garden!)

Yo no fukuru
  Hodo ōkinaru
    Hotaru kana!

(Ever as the night grows [deeper, the light of] the firefly also grows [brighter]!)

Kusakari no
  Sodé yori idzuru,
    Hotaru kana!

(See! a firefly flies out of the sleeve of the grass-cutter!)

Koko kashiko,
  Hotaru ni aoshi
    Yoru no kusa.

(Here and there the night-grass appears green, because of the light of the fireflies.)

Chōchin no
  Kiyété, tōtoki
    Hotaru kana!

(How precious seems [the light of] the firefly, now that the lantern-light has gone out!)

Fireflies

Mado kuraki,
  Shōji wo noboru
    Hotaru kana!

(The window itself is dark; but see!—a firefly is creeping up the paper pane!)

Moë yasuku,
  Mata kéyé yasuki,
    Hotaru kana!

(How easily kindled, and how easily put out again, is the light of the firefly!)

Hitotsu kite,
  Niwa no tsuyukéki,
    Hotaru kana!

(Oh! a single firefly having come, one can see the dew in the garden!)

Té no hira wo
  Hau ashi miyuru
    Hotaru kana!

(Oh, this firefly!—as it crawls on the palm of my hand, its legs are visible [by its own light]!)

Osoroshi no
  Té ni sukitoru,
    Hotaru kana!

(It is enough to make one afraid! See! the light of this firefly shows through my hand![7])

Sabeshisaya!
  Isshaku kiyete
    Yuku hotaru!

(How uncanny! The firefly shoots to within a foot of me, and—out goes the light!)

Yuku saki no
  Sawaru mono naki
    Hotaru kana!

(There goes a firefly! but there is nothing in front of it to take hold of [nothing to touch: what can it be seeking,—the ghostly creature?])

Hōki-gi ni
  Ari to wa miyété,
    Hotaru kana!

(In this hoki-bush it certainly appeared to be,—the firefly! [but where is it?])

Sodé é kité,
  Yōhan no hotaru
    Sabishi kana!

(This midnight firefly coming upon the sleeve of my robe—how weird! . . . [8])

Yanagi-ba no no
  Yami saki kaësu
    Hotaru kana!

Fireflies

(For this willow-tree the season of budding would seem to have returned in the dark,—look at the fireflies!)

Mizu soko no
　Kagé wo kowagaru
　　Hotaru kana!

(Ah, he is afraid of the darkness under the water,— that firefly! therefore he lights his tiny lantern!)

Sugitaru wa!
　Mé ni mono sugoshi
　　Tobu hotaru!

(Ah, I am going too far! . . . The flitting of the fireflies here is a lonesome sight!)

Hotarubi ya!
　Kusa ni osamaru
　　Yoäkégata.

(Ah, the firefly-lights! As the darkness begins to break, they bury themselves in the grass.)

Muréyo, hotaru,
　Mono iu kao no
　　Miyuru hodo!

(O fireflies, gather here long enough to make visible the face of the person who says these things to me![9])

Oto mo sédé,
Omoi ni moyuru,

Hotaru koso,
Naku mushi yori mo
Awaré nari-kéri!

(Not making even a sound [yet] burning with desire,—for this the firefly indeed has become more worthy of pity than any insect that cries![10])

Yū sareba,
Hotaru yori ki ni
Moyurédomo,
Hikari minéba ya
Hito no tsurénaki!

(When evening falls, though the soul of me burn more than burns the firefly, as the light [of that burning] is viewless, the person [beloved] remains unmoved.[11])

"Miscellaneous"

Suito yuku,
  Mizu-gi wa suzushi,
    Tobu-hotaru!

(Here at the water's edge, how pleasantly cool!— and the fireflies go shooting by,—suito!)

Midzu é kité,
  Hikuu naritaru
    Hotaru kana!

(Having reached the water, he makes himself low,—the firefly![12])

Fireflies

Kuzu no ha no
  Ura, utsu amé ya,
    Tobu-hotaru!

(The rain beats upon the *Kuzu*-plant;[13]—away starts the firefly from the underside of the leaf!)

Amé no yo wa,
  Shita bakari yuku
    Hotaru kana!

(Ah! this rainy night they only go along the ground,—the fireflies!)

Yura-yura to
  Ko-amé furu yo no
    Hotaru kana!

(How they swing themselves, to and fro, the fireflies, on a night of drizzling rain!)

Akinuréba,
  Kusa nomi zo
    Hotaru-kago.

(With the coming of dawn, indeed, there is nothing visible but grass in the cage of the firefly!)

Yo ga akété,
  Mushi ni naritaru
    Hotaru kana!

(With the coming of the dawn, they change into insects again,—these fireflies!)

Hiru miréba,
　　Kubi-suji akaki
　　　　Hotaru kana!

(Oh, this firefly!—seen by daylight, the nape of its neck is red!)

Hotaru kōté,
　　Shiba shi-go-mai ni
　　　　Fuzeï kana!

(Having bought fireflies, respectfully accord them the favour of four or five tufts of lawn-grass![14])

"Song of the Firefly-seller"

Futatsu, mitsu,
　　Hanashité misenu
　　　　Hotaru-uri.

Mitsu, yotsu wa,
　　Akari ni nokosé
　　　　Hotaru-uri.

Onaga mi wa
　　Yami ni kaëru ya
　　　　Hotaru-uri.

(He will not give you the chance to see two or three fireflies set free,—this firefly-seller.
He leaves in the cage three or four, just to make a light,—this firefly-seller.
For now he must take his own body back into the dark night,—this firefly-seller.)

Fireflies

VII.

But the true romance of the firefly is to be found neither in the strange fields of Japanese folk-lore nor in the quaint gardens of Japanese poetry, but in the vast profound of science. About science I know little or nothing. And that is why I am not afraid to rush in where angels fear to tread. If I knew what Professor Watasé knows about fireflies, I should feel myself less free to cross the boundaries of relative experience. As it is, I can venture theories.

The tremendous hypotheses of physical and psychical evolution no longer seem to me hypotheses: I should never dream of doubting them. I have ceased to wonder at the growth of Life out of that which has been called not-living,—the development of organic out of inorganic existence. The one amazing fact of organic evolution, to which my imagination cannot become accustomed, is the fact that the substance of life should possess the latent capacity or tendency to build itself into complexities incomprehensible of *systematic* structure. The power of that substance to evolve radiance or electricity is not really more extraordinary than its power to evolve colour; and that a noctiluca, or a luminous centipede, or a firefly, should produce light, ought not to seem more wonderful than that a plant should produce blue or purple flowers. But the biological interpretation of the phenomenon leaves me wondering, just as much as before, at the particular miracle of the machinery by which the light is made. To find embedded in the body of the insect a microscopic working-model of everything comprised under the technical designation of an "electric plant", would not be nearly so wonderful a discovery as the discovery of what actually exists. Here is a firefly, able, with its infinitesimal dynamo, to produce a pure cold light "at one four-hundredth part of the cost of the energy expended in a candle flame"! . . . Now why should there have been evolved in the tail of this tiny creature a luminiferous mechanism at once so elaborate and so effective that our greatest physiologists and chemists are still unable to understand the operation of it, and our best electricians impotent to conceive the possibility of imitating it? Why should the living tissues crystallise or build themselves into structures of such stupefying intricacy and beauty as the visual organs of an ephemera, the electrical organs of a gymnotus, or the luminiferous organs of a firefly? . . . The very wonder of the thing forbids me to imagine gods at work: no mere god could ever contrive such a prodigy as the eye of a May-fly or the tail of a firefly.

Biology would answer thus:—"Though it is inconceivable that a structure like this should have been produced by accumulated effects of function on structure, yet it is conceivable that successive selections of favourable variations might have produced it." And no follower of Herbert Spencer is really justified in wandering farther. But I cannot rid myself of the notion that Matter, in some blind infallible way, *remembers*; and that in every unit of living substance there slumber infinite potentialities, simply because to every ultimate atom belongs the infinite and indestructible experience of billions of billions of vanished universes.

Notes

[1] Professor Watasé is a graduate of Johns Hopkins. Since this essay was written, his popular Japanese lectures upon the firefly have been reissued in a single pretty volume. The coloured frontispiece,—showing fireflies at night upon a willow-branch,—is alone worth the price of the book.

Fireflies

[2] By the old calendar. According to the new calendar, the date of the Firefly Battle would be considerably later: last year (1901) it fell upon the tenth day of the sixth month.

[3] The term "*kagar-bi*", often translated by "bonfire", here especially refers to the little wood-fires which are kindled, on certain festival occasions, in front of every threshold in the principal street of a country town, or village. During the festival of the Bon such little fires are lighted in many parts of the country to welcome the returning ghosts.

[4] That is to say, "Do I see only fireflies drifting with the current? Or is the Night itself drifting, with its swarming of stars?"

[5] More literally: "The water-grasses having appeared to grow dark, the fireflies begin to fly." The phrase "*kururu to miété*" reminds one of the second stanza in that most remarkable of modern fairy-ballads, Mr. Yeats's "Folk of the Air":-

> And he saw how the weeds grew dark
> At the coming of night-tide;
> And he dreamed of the long dim hair
> Of Bridget his bride.

[6] *Oku-no-ma* really means the back room. But the best rooms in a Japanese house are always in the rear, and so arranged as to overlook the garden. The composer of the verse is supposed to be a guest at some banquet, during which fireflies are set free in the garden that the visitors may enjoy the spectacle.

[7] That is to say, makes the fingers appear diaphanous, as if held before a bright candle-flame. This suggestion of rosy semi-transparency implies a female speaker.

[8] The word "*sabishi*" usually signifies lonesome or melancholy; but the sense of it here is "weird". This verse suggests the popular fancy that the soul of a person, living or dead, may assume the form of a firefly.

[9] The speaker here is supposed to be a woman. Somebody has been making love to her in the dark; and she half doubts the sincerity of the professed affection.

[10] From the *Fugetsu-Shū*. The speaker is a woman; by the simile of the silent-glowing firefly she suggests her own secret love.

[11] From the *Kokon Wakashū Enkyō*. The speaker is supposed to be a woman.

[12] Or, "he stoops low". The word "*hikui*" really means low of stature.

[13] A kind of arrowroot.

[14] Not literal; and I doubt whether this poem could be satisfactorily translated into English. There is a delicate humour in the use of the word "*fuzei*", used in speaking humbly of one's self, or of one's endeavours to please a superior.

蜻蛉
Dragon-flies

I.

One of the old names of Japan is Akitsushima, meaning "The Island of the Dragon-fly", and written with the character representing a dragon-fly,—which insect, now called *tombō*, was anciently called *akitsu*. Perhaps this name Akitsushima, "Island of the Dragon-fly", was phonetically suggested by a still older name for Japan, also pronounced Akitsushima, but written with different characters, and signifying "The Land of Rich Harvests". However this may be, there is a tradition that the Emperor Jimmu, some twenty-six hundred years ago, ascended a mountain to gaze over the province of Yamato, and observed to those who accompanied him that the configuration of the land was like a dragon-fly licking its tail. Because of this august observation the province of Yamato came to be known as the Land of the Dragon-fly; and eventually the name was extended to the whole island. And the dragon-fly remains an emblem of the Empire even to this day.

In a literal sense, Japan well deserves to be called the Land of the Dragon-fly; for, as Rein poetically declared, it is "a true Eldorado to the neuroptera-fancier". Probably no other country of either temperate zone possesses so many kinds of dragon-flies; and I doubt whether even the tropics can produce any dragon-flies more curiously beautiful than

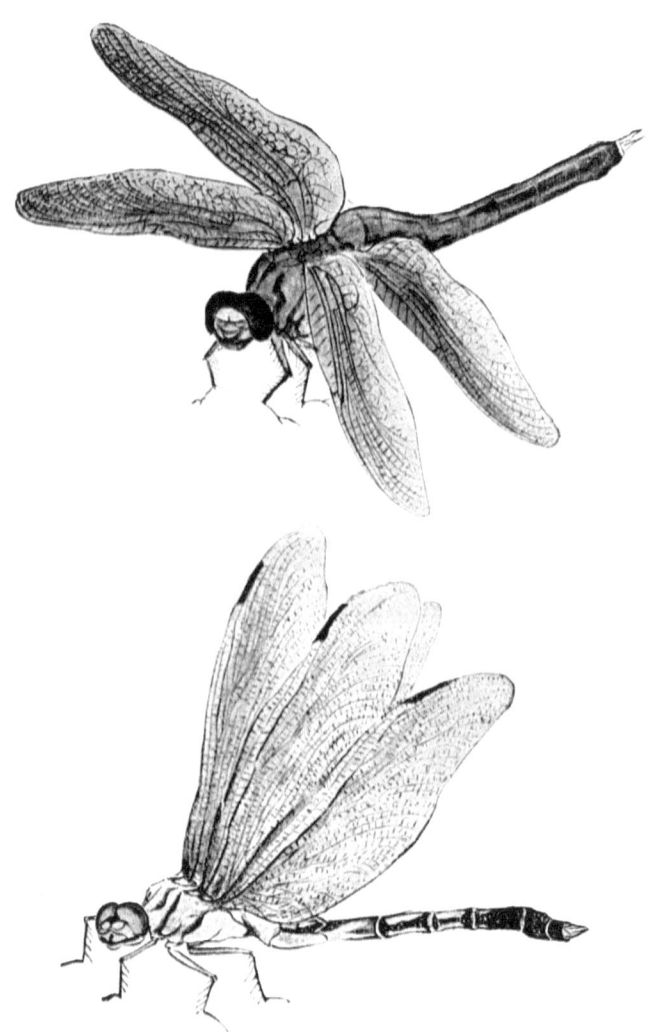

some of the Japanese species. The most wonderful dragon-fly that I ever saw was a Japanese *Calepteryx*, which I captured last summer in Shidzuoka. It was what the country-folk call a "black dragon-fly"; but the colour was really a rich deep purple. The long narrow wings, velvety purple, seemed—even to touch—like the petals of some marvellous flower. The purple body, slender as a darning-needle, was decorated with dotted lines of dead gold. The head and thorax were vivid gold-green; but the eyes were pure globes of burnished gold. The legs were fringed on the inner side with indescribably delicate spines, set at right angles to the limb, like the teeth of a fairy-comb. So exquisite was the creature that I felt a kind of remorse for having disturbed it,—felt as if I had been meddling with something belonging to the gods;—and I quickly returned it to the shrub on which it had been reposing . . . This particular kind of dragon-fly is said to haunt only the neighbourhood of a clear stream near the town of Yaidzu. It is, however, but one of many lovely varieties.

But the more exquisite dragon-flies are infrequently seen; and they seldom figure in Japanese literature;—and I can attempt to interest my reader only in the poetry and the folklore of dragon-flies. I propose to discourse of dragonflies in the old-fashioned Japanese way; and the little that I have been able to learn upon the subject,—with the help of quaint books and of long-forgotten drawings,—mostly relates to the commoner species.

But before treating of dragon-fly literature, it will be necessary to say something regarding dragon-fly nomenclature. Old Japanese books profess to name about fifty kinds; and the *Chūfu-Zusétsu* actually contains coloured pictures of nearly that number of dragon-flies. But in these volumes several insects resembling dragon-flies are improperly classed with dragon-flies; and in more than one case it would seem that different names have been given to the male and female of the same species. On the other hand I find as many as four different varieties of dragon-fly bearing the same folk-name! And in view of these facts I venture to think that the following list will be found sufficiently complete:—

I.—*Mugiwara-tombō* (or simply, *tombō*), "Barley-straw Dragon-fly",—so called because its body somewhat resembles in shape and colour a barley-straw.—This is perhaps the most common of all the dragon-flies, and the first to make its appearance.

II.—*Shiokara-tombō*, or *Shio-tombō*,—"Saltfish Dragon-fly", or "Salt Dragon-fly",—so called because the end of its tail looks as if it had been dipped in salt. *Shiokara* is the name given to a preparation of fish preserved in salt.

III.—*Kino-tombō*, "Yellow Dragon-fly".—It is not all yellow, but reddish, with yellow stripes and bands.

IV.—*Ao-tombō*. *Ao* means either blue or green; and two different kinds of dragon-fly, one green, and one metallic-blue,—are called by this name.

V.—*Koshiaki-tombō*,—"Shining Loins". The insect usually so called is black and yellow.

VI.—*Tono-Sama-tombō*,—"August-Lord Dragon-fly". Many different kinds of dragon-fly are called by this name,—probably on account of their beautiful colours. The name *Koshiaki*, or "Shining Loins", is likewise given to several varieties.

VII.—*Ko-mugi-tombō*, "Wheat-straw Dragon-fly".—Somewhat smaller than the "Barley-straw dragon-fly".

VIII.—*Tsumaguro-tombō*, "Black-skirted (or "black-hemmed") Dragon-fly".—Several kinds of dragon-flies are thus called, because the edges of the wings are black or dark-red.

Dragon-flies

IX.—*Kuro-tombō*, "Black Dragon-fly". As the word *kuro* means either dark in colour or black, it is not surprising to find this name given both to deep red and to deep purple insects.

X.—*Karakasa-tombō*, "Umbrella Dragon-fly". The body of this creature is said to resemble, both in form and colour, a closed umbrella of the kind known as *karakasa*, made of split bamboo covered with thick oil-paper.

XI.—*Chō-tombō*,—"Butterfly Dragon-fly". Several varieties of dragon-fly are thus called, apparently because of wing-markings like those of moths or butterflies.

XII.—*Shōjō-tombō*. A bright-red dragon-fly is so named, simply because of its tint.—In the zoological mythology of China and Japan, the *Shōjō* figures as a being less than human, but more than animal,—in appearance resembling a stout boy with long crimson hair. From this crimson hair it was alleged that a wonderful red dye could be extracted. The *Shōjō* was supposed to be very fond of *saké*; and in Japanese art the creature is commonly represented as dancing about a *saké*-vessel.

XIII.—*Haguro-tombō*, "Black-winged Dragon-fly".

XIV.—*Oni-yamma*, "Demon Dragon-fly". This is the largest of all the Japanese dragonflies. It is rather unpleasantly coloured; the body being black, with bright yellow bands and stripes.

XV.—*Ki-yamma*, "Goblin Dragon-fly". Also called *Ki-Emma*,— "Emma", or "*Yemma*", being the name of the King of Death and Judge of Souls.

XVI.—*Shōryō-tombō*, "The Dragon-fly of the Ancestral Spirits". This appellation, as well as another of kindred meaning,—*Shōrai-tombō*, or "Dragon-fly of the Dead",— would appear, so far as I could learn, to be given to many kinds of dragon-fly.

XVII.—*Yūrei-tombō*,—"Ghost Dragon-fly". Various creatures are called by this name,—which I thought especially appropriate in the case of one beautiful *Calepteryx*, whose soundless black flitting might well be mistaken for the motion of a shadow,—the shadow of a dragon-fly. Indeed this appellation for the black insect must have been intended to suggest the primitive idea of shadow as ghost.

XVIII.—*Kané-tsuké-tombō*, or *O-haguro-tombō*. Either name refers to the preparation formerly used to blacken the teeth of married women, and might be freely rendered as "Tooth-blackening dragon-fly". *O-haguro* ("honourable tooth-blackening") or *Kané*, were the terms by which the tooth-staining infusion was commonly known. *Kané-wo-tsukéru* signified to apply, or, more literally, *to wear* the stuff: thus the appellation *Kané-tsuké-tombō* might be interpreted as "the *Kané*-stained dragon-fly". The wings of the insect are half-black, and look as if they had been partly dipped in ink. Another and equally picturesque name for the creature is *Kōya*, "the Dyer".

XIX.—*Ta-no-Kami-tombō*, "Dragon-fly of the God of Rice-fields". This appellation has been given to an insect variegated with red and yellow.

XX.—*Yanagi-jorō*, "The Lady of the Weeping-willow". A beautiful, but ghostly name; for the *Yanagi-jorō* is the Spirit of the Willow-tree. I find that two very graceful species of dragon-fly are thus called.

XXI.—*Seki-i-Shisha*, "Red-robed Messenger".

XXII.—*Yamma-tombō*. The name is a sort of doublet; *yamma* signifying a large dragon-fly, and *tombō* any sort of dragon-fly. This is the name for a black-and-green insect, called *Onjō* in Izumo.

XXIII.—*Kuruma-yamma*, "Wagon Dragon-fly",—probably so-named from the disk-like appendages of the tail.

Dragon-flies

XXIV.—*Aka-tombō*, "Red Dragon-fly". The name is now given to various species; but the insect especially referred to as *Aka-tombō* by the old poets is a small dragon-fly, which is often seen in flocks.

XXV.—*Tōsumi-tombō*, "Lamp-wick Dragon-fly". A very small creature,—thus named because of the resemblance of its body to the slender pith-wick used in the old-fashioned Japanese lamp.

XXVI.—*Mono-sashi-tombō*, "Foot-measure Dragon-fly". This also is a very small insect. The form of its body, with the ten joint-markings, suggested this name;—the ordinary Japanese foot-measure, usually made of bamboo, being very narrow, and divided into only ten *sun*, or inches.

XXVII.—*Beni-tombō*. This is the name given to a beautiful pink dragon-fly, on account of its colour. *Beni* is a kind of rouge, with which the Japanese girl tints her lips and cheeks on certain occasions.

XXVIII.—*Mékura-tombō*, "Blind Dragon-fly". The creature thus called is not blind at all; but it dashes its large body in so clumsy a way against objects in a room that it was at one time supposed to be sightless.

XXIX.—*Ka-tombō*, "Mosquito Dragon-fly",—perhaps in the same sense as the American term "mosquito-hawk".

XXX.—*Kuro-yama-tombō*, "Black Mountain Dragon-fly",—so called to distinguish it from the *Yama-tombō*, or "Mountain Dragon-fly", which is mostly green.

XXXI.—*Ko-yama-tombō*, "Little Mountain Dragon-fly",—the name of a small insect resembling the *Yama-tombō* in form and colour.

XXXII.—*Tsuketé-dan*. The word *dan* is a general term for variegated woven stuffs; and the name *tsuketé-dan* might be freely rendered as "The Wearer of the Many-Coloured Robe".

I believe that in the foregoing list the only name requiring further explanation is the name *Shōrai-tombō*, or *Shōryō-tombō*, in its meaning of "the dragon-fly of the Dead". Unlike the equally weird name *Yurei-tombō*, or "Ghost Dragon-fly", the term *Shōrai-tombō* does not refer to the appearance of the insect, but to the strange belief that certain dragon-flies *are ridden by the dead*,—used as winged steeds. From the morning of the thirteenth to the midnight of the fifteenth day of the old seventh month, the time of the Festival of the Bon,—the dragon-flies are said to carry the *Hotoké-Sama*, the August Spirits of the Ancestors, who then revisit their former homes. Therefore during this Buddhist "All-Souls", children are forbidden to molest any dragon-flies,—especially dragon-flies that may then happen to enter the family dwelling. This supposed relation of dragon-flies to the supernatural world helps to explain an old folk saying, still current in some provinces, to the effect that the child who catches dragon-flies will never "obtain knowledge". Another curious belief is that certain dragon-flies "carry the image of Kwannon-Sama (Āvalokitesvara)",—because the markings upon the backs of the insects bear some faint resemblance to the form of a Buddhist icon.

II.

Different kinds of dragon-fly show themselves at different periods; and the more beautiful species, with few exceptions, are the latest to appear. All Japanese dragon-flies have been grouped by old writers into four classes, according to the predominant colour of each variety,—the Yellow, Green (or Blue), Black (or Dark), and Red Dragon-flies. It is said that the yellow-marked insects are the earliest to appear; that the green, blue, and black varieties first show

Dragon-flies

themselves in the Period of Greatest Heat; and that the red kinds are the last to come and the last to go,—vanishing only with the close of autumn. In a vague and general way, these statements can be accepted as results of observation. Nevertheless, the dragon-fly is popularly spoken of as a creature of autumn: indeed one of its many names, *Akitsu-mushi*, signifies "autumn insect". And the appellation is really appropriate; for it is not until the autumn that dragon-flies appear in such multitude as to compel attention. For the poet, however, the true dragon-fly of autumn is the red dragon-fly:—

Aki no kino
　Aka-tombō ni
　　Sadamarinu.

(That the autumn season has begun is decided by the [*appearance of the*] red dragon-fly.)

Onoga mini
　Aki wo sonénuku
　　Tombō kana!

(O the dragon-fly!—he has dyed his own body with [the colour of] autumn!)

Aki no hi no
　Sonéta iro nari
　　Aka-tombō!

(Dyed he is with the colour of autumn days—O the red dragon-fly!)

"Spring," says a Japanese poet, "is the Season of the Eyes; Autumn is the Season of the Ears,"—meaning that in spring the blossoming of the trees and the magic of morning haze make delight for the eyes, and that in autumn the ears are charmed by the music of countless insects. But he goes on to say that this pleasure of autumn is toned with melancholy. Those plaintive voices evoke the memory of vanished years and of vanished faces, and so to Buddhist thought recall the doctrine of impermanency. Spring is the period of promise and of hope; autumn, the time of remembrance and of regret. And the coming of autumn's special insect, the soundless dragon-fly,—voiceless in the season of voices,—only makes weirder the aspects of change. Everywhere you see a silent play of fairy lightnings,—flashes of colour continually intercrossing, like a weaving of interminable enchantment over the face of the land. Thus an old poet describes it:—

Kurénai no
　Kagerō hashiru,
　　Tombō kana!

(Like a fleeting of crimson gossamer-threads, the flashing of the dragon-flies.)

III.

For more than ten centuries the Japanese have been making verses about dragon-flies; and the subject remains a favourite one even with the younger poets of to-day. The oldest extant poem about a dragon-fly is said to have been composed, fourteen hundred and forty years ago, by the Emperor Yūriaku. One day while this Emperor was hunting, say the ancient records, a gadfly came and bit his arm.

Dragon-flies

Therewith a dragon-fly pounced upon that gadfly, and devoured it. Then the Emperor commanded his ministers to make an ode in praise of that dragon-fly. But as they hesitated how to begin, he himself composed a poem in praise of the insect, ending with the words,—

> Even a creeping insect
> Waits upon the Great Lord:
> Thy form it will bear,
> O Yamato, land of the dragon-fly!

And in honour of the loyal dragon-fly, the place of the incident was called Akitsuno, or the Moor of the Dragon-fly.

The poem attributed to the Emperor Yūriaku is written in the form called *naga-uta*, or "long poetry"; but the later poems on dragon-flies are mostly composed in the briefer forms of Japanese verse. There are three brief forms,— the ancient *tanka*, consisting of thirty-one syllables; the popular *dodoitsu*, consisting of twenty-six syllables; and the *hokku*, consisting of only seventeen. The vast majority of dragon-fly poems are in *hokku*. There are scarcely any poems upon the subject in *dodoitsu*, and—strange to say!—but very few in the classical *tanka*. The friend who collected for me all the verses quoted in this essay, and many hundreds more, declares that he read through *fifty-two volumes* of thirty-one-syllable poetry in the Imperial Library before he succeeded in finding a single composition about dragon-flies; and eventually, after much further research, he was able to discover only about a dozen such poems in *tanka*.

The reason for this must be sought in the old poetical conventions. Japanese thirty-one syllable poetry is composed according to rules that have been fixed for hundreds of years. These rules require that almost every subject treated shall be considered in some relation to one of the seasons. And this should be done in accordance with certain laws of grouping,—long established conventions of association, recognised both in painting and in poetry: for example, the nightingale should be mentioned, or portrayed, together with the plum-tree; the sparrow, with the bamboo; the cuckoo, with the moon; frogs, with rain; the butterfly, with flowers; the bat, with the willow-tree. Every Japanese child knows something about these regulations. Now, it so happens that no such relations have been clearly fixed for the dragon-fly in *tanka*-poetry,—though in pictures we often see it perched on the edge of a water-bucket, or upon an ear of ripened rice. Moreover, in the classification of subject-groupings for poetry, the dragon-fly is not placed among *mushi* ("insect"—by which word the poet nearly always means a musical insect of some sort), but among *zō*,—a term of very wide signification; for it includes the horse, cat, dog, monkey, crow, sparrow, tortoise, snake, frog,—almost all fauna, in short.

Thus the rarity of *tanka*-poems about dragon-flies may be explained. But why should dragon-flies be almost ignored in *dodoitsu*? Probably for the reason that this form of verse is usually devoted to the subject of love. The voiceless dragon-fly can suggest to the love-poet no such fancies as those inspired by the singing-insects,—especially by those night-crickets whose music lingers in the memory of some evening tryst. Out of several hundred dragon-fly poems collected for me, I find only seven relating, directly or indirectly, to the subject of love; and not one of the seven is in twenty-six-syllable verse.

But in the form *hokku*—limited to seventeen syllables—the poems on dragon-flies are almost as numerous as are the dragon-flies themselves in the early autumn. For in this measure there are few restraints placed upon

Dragon-flies

the composer, either as to theme or method. Almost the only rule about *hokku*,—not at all a rigid one,—is that the poem shall be a little word-picture,—that it shall revive the memory of something seen or felt,—that it shall appeal to some experience of sense. The greater number of the poems that I am going to quote certainly fulfil this requirement: the reader will find that they are really pictures,—tiny colour-prints in the manner of the *Ukiyoyé* school. Indeed almost any of the following could be delightfully imaged, with a few touches of the brush, by some Japanese master:—

"Picture-Poems about Dragon-flies"

Iné no ho no
   Tombō tomari
      Tarénikéri.

(An ear of rice has bent because a dragon-fly perched upon it.)

Tombō no
   Éda ni tsuitari
      Wasuré-guwa.

(See the dragon-fly resting on the handle of the forgotten mattock.[1])

Tombō no
   Kaidé yukikéri
      Suté waraji.

(Dragon-flies have gone to sniff at a pair of cast-off sandals of straw.)

Sodé ni tsuku
  Sumi ka?—obana ni
    Kané-tombō

(Is it an ink-stain upon a sleeve?—no: it is only the black dragon-fly resting upon the obana.[2])

Hi wa namamé
  Sékiya no yari ni
    Tombō kana!

(See the dragon-fly perching on the blade of the spear leaning against the rampart-wall!)

Tombō no
  Kusa ni undéya,
    Ushi no tsuno!

(O dragon-fly! how have you wearied of the grass that you should thus perch upon the horn of a cow!)

Kaki-daké no
  Ippon nagaki—
    Tombō kana!

(One of the bamboo-stakes in that fence seems to be higher than the others—but no! there is a dragon-fly upon it!)

Kaki-daké to
  Tombō to utsuru
    Shōji kana!

Dragon-flies

(The shadow of the bamboo-fence, with a dragon-fly at rest upon it, is thrown upon my paper-window!)

Tsurigané ni
Hito-toki yasumi
Tombō kana!

(See! the dragon-fly is resting awhile upon the temple bell!)

O wo motté
Kané ni mukaëru,—
Tombō kana!

(Only with his tail he thinks to oppose [the weight of] the great temple-bell,—O silly dragon-fly!)

Naki-hito no
Shirushi no také ni
Tombō kana!

(Lo! a dragon-fly rests upon the bamboo that marks the grave!)

Itte wa kité
Tombō taëzu
Funé no tsuna.

(About the ropes of the ship the dragon-flies cease not to come and go.)

Tombō ya
Funé wa nagarété
Todomarazu.

(The dragon-fly ceases not to flit about the vessel drifting down the stream.)

Tombō ya!
  Hobashira até ni
    Tōku yuku.

(O the dragon-fly!—keeping an eye upon the mast, he ventures far!)

Tombō ya!
  Hi no kagé dékité,
    Nami no uë.

(Poor dragon-fly!—now that the sun has become obscured, he wanders over the waves.)

Wata-tori no
  Kasa ya tombō no
    Hitotsu-zutsu.

(Look at the bamboo-hats of the cotton-pickers!— there is a dragon-fly perched on each of them!)

Nagaré-yuku
  A wa ni yumé miru
    Tombō kana!

(Lo! the dragon-fly dreams a dream above the flowing of the foam-bubbles!)

Uki-kusa no
  Hana ni asobu ya,
    Aka-tombō!

Dragon-flies

(See the red dragon-fly sporting about the blossoms of the water-weed!)

Tombō no
  Hitoshio akashi
    Fuchi no uë.

(Much more red seems the red dragon-fly when hovering above the pool.)

Tsuri-betá no
  Sao ni kité néru
    Tombō kana!

(See! the dragon-fly settles down to sleep on the rod of the unskilful angler.)

Tombō no
  Ha-ura ni sabishi,—
    Aki-shiguré.

(Lonesomely clings the dragon-fly to the underside of the leaf—Ah! the autumn-rains!)

Tombō no
  Tō bakari tsuku
    Kara-é kana!

(Only ten dragon-flies—all clinging to the same withered spray!)

Yosogoto no
  Naruko ni nigéru,
    Tombō kana!

(Poor dragon-fly! scared away by the clapper[3] that never was intended for you!)

Ao-zora ya,
  Ka hodo mure-tobu
    Aka-tombō.

(High in the azure sky the gathering of red dragon-flies looks like a swarming of mosquitoes.)

Furu-haka ya;
  Aka-tombō tobu;
    Karé shikimi.

(Old tomb!—[only] a flitting of red dragon-flies;—some withered [offerings of] shikimi[4] [before the grave]!)

Sabishisa wo!
  Tombō tobu nari
    Haka no uë.

(Desolation!—dragon-flies flitting above the graves!)

Tombō tonde,
  Koto-naki mura no
    Hi go nari.

(Dragon-flies are flitting, and the noon-sun is shining, above the village where nothing eventful ever happens.)

Dragon-flies

Yūzuki hi
  Usuki tombō no
    Ha-kagé kana!

(O the thin shadow of the dragon-fly's wings in the light of sunset!)

Tombō no
  Kabé wo kakayuru
    Nishi-hi kana!

(O that sunlight from the West, and the dragon-fly clinging to the wall!)

Tombō toru
  Iri-hi ni tori no
    Métsuki kana!

(O the expression of that cock's eyes in the sunset-light—trying to catch a dragon-fly!)

Tombō no
  Mo ya iri-hi no
    Issékai.

(Dance, O dragon-flies, in your world of the setting sun!)

Nama-kabé ni
  Yū-hi sasunari
    Aka-tombō.

(To the freshly-plastered wall a red dragon-fly clings in the light of the setting-sun.[5])

Déru tsuki to
  Iri-hi no ai ya—
    Aka-tombō.

(In the time between the setting of the sun and the rising of the moon—red dragon-flies.)

Yū-kagé ya,
  Nagaré ni hitasu
    Tombō no o!

(The dragon-fly at dusk dips her tail into the running stream.)

IV.

The foregoing compositions are by old authors mostly: few modern *hokku* on the subject have the same naïve quality of picturesqueness. The older poets seem to have watched the ways of the dragon-fly with a patience and a freshness of curiosity impossible to this busier generation. They made verses about all its habits and peculiarities,—even about such matters as the queer propensity of the creature to return many times in succession to any spot once chosen for a perch. Sometimes they praised the beauty of its wings, and compared them to the wings of devas or Buddhist angels; sometimes they celebrated the imponderable grace of its hovering,—the ghostly stillness and lightness of its motion; and sometimes they jested about its waspish appearance of anger, or about the goblin oddity of its stare. They noticed the wonderful way in which it can change the direction of its course, or reverse the play of its wings with the sudden turn that suggested the modern Japanese word for a somersault,—*tombōgaëri* ("dragon-fly-turning").[6] In the dazzling rapidity of its flight—invisible but as a needle-gleam of darting colour—they found a similitude for impermanency. But they perceived that this lightning flight was of short duration, and that the dragon-fly seldom travels far, unless pursued, preferring to flit about one spot all day long. Some thought it worth while to record in verse that at sunset all the dragonflies flock towards the glow, and that they rise high in air when the sun sinks below the horizon,—as if they hoped to obtain from the altitudes one last sight of the vanishing splendour. They remarked that the dragon-fly cares nothing for flowers, and is apt to light upon stakes or stones rather than upon blossoms; and they wondered what pleasure it could find in resting on the rail of a fence or upon the horn of a cow. Also they marvelled at its stupidity when attacked with sticks or stones,—as often flying toward the danger as away from it. But they sympathized with its struggles in the spider's net, and rejoiced to see it burst through the meshes. The following examples, selected from hundreds of compositions, will serve to suggest the wide range of these curious studies:—

"Dragon-flies and Sunshine"

Tombō ya,
　Hi no sasu kataë
　　Taté-yuku!

(O dragon-fly! ever towards the sun you rise and soar!)

Hiatari no
　Doté ya hinémosu
　　Tombō tobu.

(Over the sunlit bank, all day long, the dragon-flies flit to and fro.)

Go-roku shaku
  Onoga kumoi no
    Tombō kana!

(Poor dragon-fly!—the [blue] space of five or six feet [above him] he thinks to be his own sky!)

Tombō no
  Muki wo soroëru
    Nishi-hi kana!

(Ah, the sunset-glow! Now all the dragon-flies are shooting in the same direction.)

Tombō ya!
  Sora é hanarété
    Kurékakari.

(Dusk approaches: see! the dragon-flies have risen toward the sky!)

Hoshi hitotsu
  Miru madé asobu
    Tombō kana!

(O dragon-fly! you continue to sport until the first star appears!)

Tō yama ya,
  Tombō tsui-yuki,
    Tsui-kaëru.

Dragon-flies

(Quickly the dragon-fly starts for the distant mountain, but as quickly returns.)

Yukiōté,
  Dochiramo soréru
    Tombō kana!

(Meeting in flight, how wonderfully do the dragon-flies glance away from each other!)

Narabu ka to
  Miété wa soréru
    Tombō kana!

(Lo! the dragon-flies that seemed to fly in line all scatter away from each other.)

"Mentioned in Love-Songs"

Kagérō no
  Kagé tomo waré wa
    Nari ni keri
Aruka nakika no
  Kimi ga nasaké ni.

(Even as the shadow of a dragon-fly[7] I have become, by reason of the slightness of your love.)

Obotsu kana!
  Yumé ka? utsusu ka?
    Kagérō no
Honoméku yori mo
  Hakanakarishi wa!

(O my doubt! Is it a dream or a reality?—more fugitive than even the dim flitting of a dragon-fly![8])

Tombō ya!
  Mi wo mo kogasazu,
    Naki mo sézu!

(Happy dragon-fly!—never self-consumed by longing, never even uttering a cry!)

"Strangeness and Beauty"

Tombō no
  Kao wa ōkata
    Médama kana!

(O the face of the dragon-fly!—almost nothing but eyes!)

Koë naki wo,
  Tombō munen ni
    Miyuru kana!

(O dragon-fly! you appear to be always angry because you have no voice!)

Sémi ni makénu
  Hagoromo mochishi,
    Tombō kana!

(O dragon-fly! the celestial raiment[9] you possess is nowise inferior to that of the cicada!)

Dragon-flies

"Lightness of Dragon-flies"

Tsubamé yori
  Tombō wa mono mo
    Ugokasazu.

(More lightly even than the swallow does the dragon-fly touch things without moving them.)

Tombō ya,
  Tori no fumarénu
    Éda no saki!

(O dragon-fly, you perch on the tip of the spray where never a bird can tread!)

"Stupidity of Dragon-flies"

Utsu-tsuë no
  Saki ni tomarishi,
    Tombō kana!

(O dragon-fly! you light upon the end of the very stick with which one tries to strike you down!)

Tachi-kaëru
  Tombō tomaru
    Tsubuté kana!

(See! the dragon-fly returns to perch upon the pebble that was thrown at it!)

"Dragon-flies and Spiders"

Kumonosu no
  Atari ni asobu
    Tombō kana!

(Ah! the poor dragon-fly, sporting beside the spider's web!)

Sasagami no
  Ami no hazurété,
    Tombō kana!

(Good dragon-fly!—he has extricated himself from the net of the spider!)

Kumo gaki mo
  Yaburu kihoi ya,
    Oni-tombō!

(Through even the spider's fence he has force to burst his way!—O the demon-dragon-fly!)

"Heedless of Flowers"

Tombō ya!
  Hana-no ni mo mé wa
    Hosorasézu.

(Ah, the dragon-fly! even in the flower-field he never half-shuts his eyes![10])

Tombō ya!
  Hana ni wa yoradé,

Dragon-flies

Ishi no uë.

(O the dragon-fly!—heedless of the flowers, he lights upon a stone!)

Tombō ya!
  Hana naki kui ni
    Sumi-narai.

(Ah, the dragon-fly! content to dwell upon a flowerless stake!)

Néta ushi no
  Tsuno ni hararénu,
    Yamma kana!

(O great dragon-fly! will you never leave the horn of the sleeping ox?)

Kui no saki
  Nanika ajiwō
    Tombō kana?

(O dragon-fly! what can you be tasting on the top of that fence-stake?)

Of course these compositions make but slight appeal to aesthetic sentiment: they are merely curious, for the most part. But they help us to understand something of the soul of the elder Japan. The people who could find delight, century after century, in watching the ways of insects, and in making such verses about them, must have comprehended, better than we, the simple pleasure of existence. They could not, indeed, describe the magic of nature as our great Western poets have done; but they could feel the beauty of the world without its sorrow, and rejoice in that beauty, much after the manner of inquisitive and happy children.

If they could have seen the dragon-fly as we can see it,—if they could have looked at that elfish head with its jewelled ocelli, its marvellous compound eyes, its astonishing mouth, under the microscope,—how much more extraordinary would the creature have seemed to them! . . . And yet, though wise enough to have lost that fresh naïve pleasure in natural observation which colours the work of these quaint poets, we are not so very much wiser than they were in regard to the real wonder of the insect. We are able only to estimate more accurately the immensity of our ignorance concerning it. Can we ever hope for a Natural History with coloured plates that will show us how the world appears to the faceted eyes of a dragon-fly?

V.

Catching dragon-flies has been for hundreds of years a favourite amusement of Japanese children. It begins with the hot season, and lasts during the greater part of the autumn. There are many old poems about it,—describing the recklessness of the little hunters. To-day, just as in other centuries, the excitement of the chase leads them into all sorts of trouble: they tumble down embankments, and fall into ditches, and scratch and dirty themselves most fearfully,— heedless of thorns or mud-holes or quagmires,—heedless of heat,—heedless even of the dinner-hour:—

Méshi-doki mo
 Modori wasurété,
  Tombō-tsuri!

Dragon-flies

(Even at the hour of the noon-day meal they forget to return home,—the children catching dragon-flies!)

Hadaka-go no
　Tombō tsuri-kéri
　　Hiru no tsuji!

(The naked child has been catching dragon-flies at the road-crossing,—heedless of the noon-sun!)

But the most celebrated poem in relation to this amusement is of a touching character. It was written by the famous female poet, Chiyo of Kaga, after the death of her little boy:—

Tombō-tsuri!—
　Kyō wa doko madé
　　Itta yara!

("Catching dragon-flies! . . . I wonder where he has gone to-day!")

The verse is intended to suggest, not to express, the emotion of the mother. She sees children running after dragon-flies, and thinks of her own dead boy who used to join in the sport,—and so finds herself wondering, in presence of the infinite Mystery, what has become of the little soul. Whither has it gone?—in what shadowy play does it now find delight?

Dragon-flies are captured sometimes with nets, sometimes by means of bamboo rods smeared at the end with birdlime, sometimes even by striking them down with a light stick or switch. The use of a switch, however, is not commonly approved; for the insect is thereby maimed, and to injure it unnecessarily is thought to be unlucky,— by reason, perhaps, of its supposed relation to the dead. A very successful method of dragon-fly-catching—practised chiefly in the Western provinces—is to use a captured female dragon-fly as a decoy. One end of a long thread is fastened to the insect's tail, and the other end of the thread to a flexible rod. By moving the rod in a particular way the female can be kept circling on her wings at the full length of the thread; and a male is soon attracted. As soon as he clings to the female, a slight jerk of the rod will bring both insects into the angler's hand. With a single female for lure, it is easy to capture eight or ten males in succession.

During these dragon-fly hunts the children usually sing little songs, inviting the insect to approach. There are many such dragon-fly songs; and they differ according to province. An Izumo song of this class[11] contains a curious allusion to the traditional conquest of Korea in the third century by the armies of the Empress Jingō; the male dragon-fly being thus addressed:—*"Thou, the male, King of Korea, art not ashamed to flee from the Queen of the East?"* In Tōkyō to-day the little dragon-fly hunters usually sing the following:—

Tombō! tombō!
 O-tomari!—
Ashita no ichi ni,
Shiōkara kōté,
Néburasho!

(Dragon-fly! dragon-fly! honorably wait!— to-morrow at the market I will buy some *shiōkara* and let you lick it!)

Dragon-flies

Children also find amusement in catching the larva of the dragon-fly. This larva has many popular names; but is usually called in Tōkyō *taiko-mushi*, or "drum-insect", because it moves its forelegs in the water somewhat as a man moves his arms while playing upon a drum.

A most extraordinary device for catching dragon-flies is used by the children of the province of Kii. They get a long hair,— a woman's hair,—and attach a very small pebble to each end of it, so as to form a miniature "bolas"; and this they sling high into the air. A dragon-fly pounces upon the passing object; but the moment that he seizes it, the hair twists round his body, and the weight of the pebbles brings him to the ground. I wonder whether this method of bolassing dragon-flies is known anywhere outside of Japan.

Notes

[1] The *kuwa* is shaped like a hoe, but is a much heavier tool. When left with the heavy blade resting flat upon the ground, as suggested in this little word-picture, the handle remains almost perpendicular.

[2] *Obana* is another name for the beautiful flowering grass usually *susuki*, and known to botanists as *Eularia japonica*.

[3] *Naruko*. This clapper, used to frighten away birds from the crops, consists of a number of pieces of bamboo, or hard wood, fastened to a rope extended across the field or garden. When the end of the rope is pulled, the pieces of wood rattle loudly.

[4] It is the custom to set sprays of *shikimi* in bamboo vases before the graves of Buddhist dead. The *shikimi* is a kind of anise, botanically known as *Illicium religiosum*.

[5] This is a tiny colour-study. The tint of the freshly-plastered wall is supposed to be a warm grey.

[6] *Tombōgaëri wo utsu*, "to throw a dragon-fly-turning" is the Japanese expression corresponding with our phrase, "to turn a somersault".

[7] The word *kagérō* here means "dragon-fly". There is another word *kagérō* meaning "gossamer". Though written alike in Romaji, the two terms are represented in Japanese by very different characters.

[8] The thought suggested is,—"Can it be true that we were ever united, even for a moment?"

[9] Literally "feather-robe" (*hagoromo*);—this is the name given to the raiment supposed to be worn by the "Sky-People"—angelic inhabitants of the Buddhist heaven. The *hagoromo* enables its wearer to soar through space: and the poet compares the wings of the beautiful insect to such a fairy robe.

[10] Alluding to the fact that one half-closes one's eyes,—in order to shadow them, and to see more distinctly,—when looking at some beautiful object,—Perhaps the rendering, "never makes his eyes narrower," would better express the exact sense of the original.

[11] Cited in *Glimpses of Unfamiliar Japan*; Vol. II, p. 372.

蝉
Sémi

I.

A celebrated Chinese scholar, known in Japanese literature as Riku-Un, wrote the following quaint account of the Five Virtues of the Cicada:—

"I.—The Cicada has upon its head certain figures or signs.[1] These represent its (written) characters, style, literature.
"II.—It eats nothing belonging to earth, and drinks only dew. This proves its cleanliness, purity, propriety.
"III.—It always appears at a certain fixed time. This proves its fidelity, sincerity, truthfulness.
"IV.—It will not accept wheat or rice. This proves its probity, uprightness, honesty.
"V.—It does not make for itself any nest to live in. This proves its frugality, thrift, economy."

We might compare this with the beautiful address of Anacreon to the cicada, written twenty-four hundred years ago: on more than one point the Greek poet and the Chinese sage are in perfect accord:—

"We deem thee happy, O Cicada, because, having drunk, like a king, only a little dew, thou dost chir-

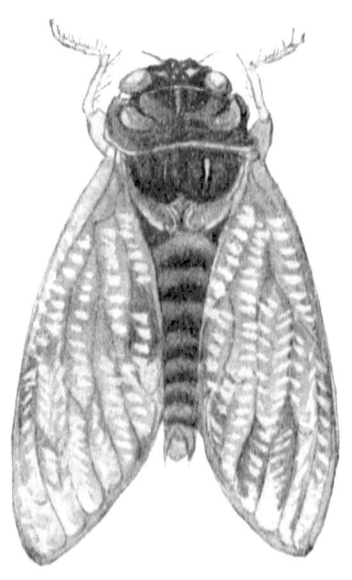
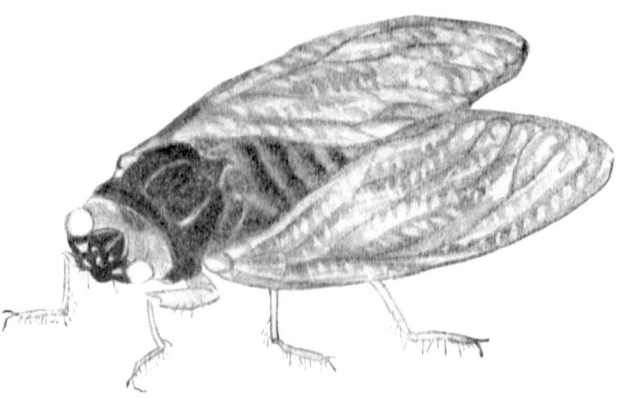

rup on the tops of trees. For all things whatsoever that thou seest in the fields are thine, and whatsoever the seasons bring forth. Yet art thou the friend of the tillers of the land,—from no one harmfully taking aught. By mortals thou art held in honour as the pleasant harbinger of summer; and the Muses love thee. Phoebus himself loves thee, and has given thee a shrill song. And old age does not consume thee. O thou gifted one,— earth-born, song-loving, free from pain, having flesh without blood,—thou art nearly equal to the Gods!" [2]

And we must certainly go back to the old Greek literature in order to find a poetry comparable to that of the Japanese on the subject of musical insects. Perhaps of Greek verses on the cricket, the most beautiful are the lines of Meleager: *"O cricket, the soother of slumber . . . weaving the thread of a voice that causes love to wander away!"* . . . There are Japanese poems scarcely less delicate in sentiment on the chirruping of night-crickets; and Meleager's promise to reward the little singer with gifts of fresh leek, and with "drops of dew cut up small", sounds strangely Japanese. Then the poem attributed to Anyté, about the little girl Myro making a tomb for her pet cicada and cricket, and weeping because Hades, "hard to be persuaded", had taken her playthings away, represents an experience familiar to Japanese child-life. I suppose that little Myro—(how freshly her tears still glisten, after seven and twenty centuries!)—prepared that "common tomb" for her pets much as the little maid of Nippon would do to-day, putting a small stone on top to serve for a monument. But the wiser Japanese Myro would repeat over the grave a certain Buddhist prayer.

It is especially in their poems upon the cicada that we find the old Greeks confessing their love of insect-melody:

witness the lines in the Anthology about the tettix caught in a spider's snare, and "making lament in the thin fetters" until freed by the poet; and the verses by Leonidas of Tarentum picturing the "unpaid minstrel to wayfaring men" as "sitting upon lofty trees, warmed with the great heat of summer, sipping the dew that is like woman's milk";—and the dainty fragment of Meleager, beginning: "*Thou vocal tettix, drunk with drops of dew, sitting with thy serrated limbs upon the tops of petals, thou givest out the melody of the lyre from thy dusky skin.*" . . . Or take the charming address of Evenus to a nightingale:—

> "*Thou Attic maiden, honey-fed, hast chirping seized a chirping cicada, and bearest it to thy unfledged young,—thou, a twitterer, the twitterer,—thou, the winged, the well-winged,—thou, a stranger, the stranger—thou, a summerchild, the summerchild! Wilt thou not quickly cast it from thee? For it is not right, it is not just, that those engaged in song should perish by the mouth of those engaged in song.*"

On the other hand, we find Japanese poets much more inclined to praise the voices of night crickets than those of sémi. There are countless poems about sémi, but very few which commend their singing. Of course the sémi are very different from the cicadae known to the Greeks. Some varieties are truly musical; but the majority are astonishingly noisy,—so noisy that their stridulation is considered one of the great afflictions of summer. Therefore it were vain to seek among the myriads of Japanese verses on sémi for anything comparable to the lines of Evenus above quoted; indeed, the only Japanese poem that I could find on the subject of a cicada caught by a bird, was the following:—

Sémi

Ana kanashi!
　Tobi ni—toraruru
　　Sémi no koë. – Ransetsu

(Ah! How piteous the cry of the sémi seized by the kite!)

Or "caught by a boy" the poet might equally well have observed,—this being a much more frequent cause of the pitiful cry. The lament of Nicias for the tettix would serve as the elegy of many a sémi:—

"No more shall I delight myself by sending out a sound from my quick-moving wings, because I have fallen into the savage hand of a boy, who seized me unexpectedly, as I was sitting under the green leaves."

Here I may remark that Japanese children usually capture sémi by means of a long slender bamboo tipped with birdlime (*mochi*). The sound made by some kinds of sémi when caught is really pitiful,—quite as pitiful as the twitter of a terrified bird. One finds it difficult to persuade oneself that the noise is not a voice of anguish, in the human sense of the word "voice", but the production of a specialised exterior membrane. Recently, on hearing a captured sémi thus scream, I became convinced in quite a new way that the stridulatory apparatus of certain insects must not be thought of as a kind of musical instrument but as an organ of speech, and that its utterances are as intimately associated with simple forms of emotion, as are the notes of a bird,—the extraordinary difference being that the insect has its vocal chords *outside*.

But the insect-world is altogether a world of goblins and fairies: creatures with organs of which we cannot discover the use, and senses of which we cannot imagine the nature;—creatures with myriads of eyes, or with eyes in their backs, or with eyes moving about at the ends of trunks and horns;—creatures with ears in their legs and bellies, or with brains in their waists! If some of them happen to have voices outside of their bodies instead of inside, the fact ought not to surprise anybody.

I have not yet succeeded in finding any Japanese verses alluding to the stridulatory apparatus of sémi,—though I think it probable that such verses exist. Certainly the Japanese have been for centuries familiar with the peculiarities of their own singing insects. But I should not now presume to say that their poets are incorrect in speaking of the "voices" of crickets and of cicadae. The old Greek poets who actually describe insects as producing music with their wings and feet, nevertheless speak of the "voices", the "songs", and the "chirruping" of such creatures,—just as the Japanese poets do. For example, Meleager thus addresses the cricket:

"O thou art with shrill wings the self-formed imitation of the lyre, chirrup me something pleasant while beating your vocal wings with your feet! . . . "

II.

Before speaking further of the poetical literature of sémi, I must attempt a few remarks about the sémi themselves. But the reader need not expect anything entomological. Excepting, perhaps, the butterflies, the insects of Japan are still little known to men of science; and all that I can say about sémi has been learned from inquiry, from personal observation, and from old Japanese books of an interesting but totally unscientific kind. Not only do the authors

Sémi

contradict each other as to the names and characteristics of the best-known sémi; they attach the word sémi to the name of insects which are not cicadae.

The following enumeration of sémi is certainly incomplete; but I believe that it includes the better known varieties and the best melodists. I must ask the reader, however, to bear in mind that the time of the appearance of certain sémi differs in different parts of Japan; that the same kind of sémi may be called by different names in different provinces; and that these notes have been written in Tōkyō.

1.—Haru-Zémi

Various small sémi appear in the spring. But the first of the big sémi to make itself heard is the *haru-zémi* ("spring-sémi") also called *uma-zémi* ("horse-sémi"), *kuma-zémi* ("bear-sémi"), and other names. It makes a shrill wheezing sound,—ji-i-i-i-i-iiiiiiii,—beginning low, and gradually rising to a pitch of painful intensity. No other cicada is so noisy as the *haru-zémi*; but the life of the creature appears to end with the season. Probably this is the sémi referred to in an old Japanese poem:

Hatsu-sémi ya!
  "Koré wa atsui" to
    Iu hi yori. – Taimu

(The day after the first day on which we exclaim "Oh, how hot it is!" The first sémi begins to cry.)

2.—Shinné-Shinné

The *shinneé-shinné*—also called *yama-zémi*, or "mountain-sémi"; *kuma-zémi*, or "bear sémi"; and ō-sémi, or "great-sémi"—begins to sing as early as May. It is a very large insect. The upper part of the body is almost black, and the belly a silvery-white; the head has curious red markings. The name *shinné-shinné* is derived from the note of the creature, which resembles a quick continual repetition of the syllables *shinné*. About Kyōto this sémi is common: it is rarely heard in Tōkyō.

(My first opportunity to examine an ō-sémi was in Shidzuoka. Its utterance is much more complex than the Japanese onomatope implies; I should liken it to the noise of a sewing machine in full operation. There is a double sound: you hear not only the succession of sharp metallic clickings, but also, below these, a slower series of dull clanking tones. The stridulatory organs are light green, looking almost like a pair of tiny green leaves attached to the thorax.)

3.—Aburazémi

The *aburazémi*, or "oil-sémi", makes its appearance early in the summer. I am told that it owes its name to the fact that its shrilling resembles the sound of oil or grease frying in a pan. Some writers say that the shrilling resembles the sound of the syllables *gacharhin-gacharin*; but others compare it to the noise of water boiling. The *aburazémi* begins to chant about sunrise; then a great soft hissing seems to ascend from all the trees. At such an hour, when the foliage of woods and gardens still sparkles with dew, might have been composed the following verse,—the only one in my collecting relating to the *aburazémi*:—

> *Ano koë dé*
>   *Tsuyu ga inochi ka?—*
>   *Aburazémi!*

Sémi

(Speaking with that voice, has the dew taken life?—
Only the *aburazémi*!)

4.—*Mugi-Kari-Zémi*

The *mugi-kari-zémi*, or "barley-harvest sémi", also called *goshiki-zémi*, or "five-colour sémi", appears early in the summer. It makes two distinct sounds in different keys, resembling the syllables *shi-in, shin—chi-i, chi-i.*

5.—*Higurashi, or "Kana-Kana"*

This insect, whose name signifies "day-darkening", is the most remarkable of all the Japanese cicadae. It is not the finest singer among them; but even as a melodist it ranks second only to the *tsuku-tsuku-bōshi*. It is the special minstrel of twilight, singing only at dawn and sunset; whereas most of the other sémi make their music only in the full blaze of day, pausing even when rainclouds obscure the sun. In Tōkyō the *higurashi* usually appears about the end of June, or the beginning of July. Its wonderful cry, *kana-kana-kana-kana-kana*, beginning always in a very high clear key, and slowly descending, is almost exactly like the sound of a good hand-bell, very quickly rung. It is not a clashing sound, as of violent ringing; it is quick, steady, and of surprising sonority. I believe that a single *higurashi* can be plainly heard a quarter of a mile away; yet, as the old Japanese poet Yayū observed, "no matter how many *higurashi* be singing together, we never find them noisy." Though powerful and penetrating as a resonance of metal, the *higurashi's* call is musical even to the degree of sweetness; and there is a peculiar melancholy in it that accords with the hour of gloaming. But the most astonishing fact in regard to the cry of the *higurashi* is the individual quality characterising the note of each insect. No two *higurashi* sing precisely in the same tone. If you hear a dozen of them singing at once, you will find that the timbre of each voice is recognisably different from every other. Certain notes ring like silver, others vibrate like bronze; and, besides varieties of timbre suggesting bells of various weight and composition, there are even differences in tone, that suggest different *forms* of bell.

I have already said that the name *higurashi* means "day-darkening",—in the sense of twilight, gloaming, dusk; and there are many Japanese verses containing plays on the word,—the poets affecting to believe, as in the following example, that the crying of the insect hastens the coming of darkness:—

Higurashi ya!
 Sutétéoitémo
  Kururu hi wo.

(O Higurashi!—even if you let it alone, day darkens fast enough!)

This, intended to express a melancholy mood, may seem to the Western reader far-fetched. But another little poem—referring to the effect of the sound upon the conscience of an idler—will be appreciated by any one accustomed to hear the *higurashi*. I may observe, in this connection, that the first clear evening cry of the insect is quite as startling as the sudden ringing of a bell:—

Higurashi ya!
 Kyō no kétai wo
  Omou-toki. – Rikei

(Already, O Higurashi, your call announces the evening! Alas, for the passing day, with its duties left undone!)

6.—"Minmin"-Zémi

The *minmin-zémi* begins to sing in the Period of Greatest Heat. It is called "*min-min*" because its note is thought to resemble the syllable "*min*" repeated over and over again,— slowly at first, and very loudly; then more and more quickly and softly, till the utterance dies away in a sort of buzz: "*min—min—min-min-min-minminmin-dzzzzzzz*". The sound is plaintive, and not unpleasing. It is often compared to the sound of the voice of a priest chanting the *sūtras*.

7.—Tsuku-Tsuku-Bōshi

On the day immediately following the Festival of the Dead, by the old Japanese calendar[3] (which is incomparably more exact than our Western calendar in regard to nature-changes and manifestations), begins to sing the *tsuku-tsuku-bōshi*. This creature may be said to sing like a bird. It is also called *kutsu-kutsu-bōshi*, *chōko-chōko-uisu*, *tsuku-tsuku-hōshi*, *tsuku-tsuku-oïshi*,—all onomatopoetic appellations. The sounds of its song have been imitated in different ways by various writers. In Izumo the common version,—

Tsuku-tsuku-uisu,
Tsuku-tsuku-uisu,
Tsuku-tsuku-uisu:—
   Ui-ōsu
   Ui-ōsu
   Ui-ōsu
   Ui-ōs-s-s-s-s-s-s-su.

Another version runs,—

Tsuku-tsuku-uisu,
Tsuku-tsuku-uisu,
Tsuku-tsuku-uisu:—
Chi-i yara!
   Chi-i yara!
   Chi-i yara!
   Chi-i, chi, chi, chi, chi, chiii.

There is a legend that in old times a man of Tsukushi (the ancient name of Kyūshū) fell sick and died while far away from home, and that the ghost of him became an autumn cicada, which cries unceasingly, *Tsukushi-koïshi!—Tsukushi-koïshi!* ("I long for *Tsukushi*! I want to see *Tsukushi*!")

It is a curious fact that the earlier sémi have the harshest and simplest notes. The musical sémi do not appear until summer; and the *tsuku-tsuku-bōshi*, having the most complex and melodious utterance of all, is one of the latest to mature.

8.—*Tsurigané-Sémi* [4]

The *tsurigané-sémi* is an autumn cicada. The word *tsurigané* means a suspended bell,—especially the big bell of a Buddhist temple. I am somewhat puzzled by the name; for the insect's music really suggests the tones of a Japanese harp, or *koto*—as good authorities declare. Perhaps the appellation refers not to the boom of the bell, but to those deep, sweet hummings which follow after the peal, wave upon wave.

Sémi

III.

Japanese poems on sémi are usually very brief; and my collection chiefly consists of *hokku*,—compositions of seventeen syllables. Most of these *hokku* relate to the sound made by the sémi,—or, rather, to the sensation which the sound produced within the poet's mind. The names attached to the following examples are nearly all names of old-time poets,—not the real names, of course, but the *gō*, or literary names by which artists and men of letters are usually known.

Yokoi Yayū, a Japanese poet of the eighteenth century, celebrated as a composer of *hokku*, has left us this naïve record of the feelings with which he heard the chirruping of cicadae in summer and in autumn:—

> "In the sultry period, feeling oppressed by the greatness of the heat, I made this verse:—

"Sémi atsushi
  Matsu kirabaya to
    Omou-madé.

> (The chirruping of the sémi aggravates the heat until I wish to cut down the pine-tree on which it sings.)

> "But the days passed quickly; and later, when I heard the crying of the sémi grow fainter and fainter in the time of the autumn winds, I began to feel compassion for them, and I made this second verse:—

"Shini-nokoré
  Hitotsu bakari wa
    Aki no sémi."

(Now there survives, but a single one of the sémi of autumn!)

Lovers of Pierre Loti (the world's greatest prose-writer) may remember in Madame Chrysanthéme a delightful passage about a Japanese house,—describing the old dry woodwork as impregnated with sonority by the shrilling crickets of a hundred summers.[5] There is a Japanese poem containing a fancy not altogether dissimilar:—

Matsu no ki ni
  Shimikomu gotoshi
    Sémi no koë.

(Into the wood of the pine-tree seems to soak the voice of the sémi.)

A very large number of Japanese poems about sémi describe the noise of the creatures as an affliction. To fully sympathise with the complaints of the poets, one must have heard certain varieties of Japanese cicadae in full midsummer chorus; but even by readers without experience of the clamour, the following verses will probably be found suggestive:—

Waré hitori
  Atsui yō nari,—
    Sémi no koë! – Bunsō

(Me seems that only I,—I alone among mortals,— Ever suffered such heat!—oh, the noise of the sémi!)

Ushiro kara
  Tsukamu yō nari,—
    Sémi no koë. – Jofū

Sémi

(Oh, the noise of the sémi!—a pain of invisible seizure,—Clutched in an enemy's grasp,—caught by the hair from behind!)

Yama no Kami no
  Mimi no yamai ka?—
    Sémi no koë. – Teikoku

(What ails the divinity's ears?—how can the God of the Mountain suffer such noise to exist?—oh, the tumult of sémi!)

Soko no nai
  Atsusa ya kumo ni
    Sémi no koë! – Saren

(Fathomless deepens the heat: the ceaseless shrilling of semi; Mounts, like a hissing of fire, up to the motionless clouds.)

Mizu karété,
  Sémi wo fudan-no
    Taki no koë. – Gen-u

(Water never a drop: the chorus of sémi, incessant, Mocks the tumultuous hiss,—the rush and foaming of rapids.)

Kagéroishi
  Kumo mata satté,
    Sémi no koë! – Kitō

(Gone, the shadowing clouds!—again the shrilling of sémi; Rises and slowly swells,—ever increasing the heat!)

Daita ki wa,
  Ha mo ugokasazu,—
    Sémi no koë! – Kafū

(Somewhere fast to the bark he clung; but I cannot see him: He stirs not even a leaf—oh! The noise of that sémi!)

Tonari kara
  Kono ki nikumu ya!
    Sémi no koë. – Gyukaku

(All because of the sémi that sit and shrill on its branches—Oh! How this tree of mine is hated now by my neighbour!)

This reminds one of Yayū. We find another poet compassionating a tree frequented by sémi:—

Kaze wa mina
  Sémi ni suwarete,
    Hito-ki kana! – Chōsui

(Alas! poor solitary tree!—pitiful now your lot,—every breath of air having been sucked up by the sémi!)

Sometimes the noise of the sémi is described as a moving force:—

Sémi no koë
  Ki-gi ni ugoite
    Kaze mo nashi! – Sōyō

Sémi

(Every tree in the wood quivers with clamour of sémi: Motion only of noise—never a breath of wind!)

Také ni kite,
 Yuki yori omoshi
  Sémi no koë. – Tōgetsu

(More heavy than winter-snow the voices of perching sémi: See how the bamboos bend under the weight of their song![6])

Morogoë ni
 Yama ya ugokasu,
  Ki-gi no sémi.

(All shrilling together, the multitudinous semi; Make, with their ceaseless clamour, even the mountain move.)

Kusinoki mo
 Ugoku yō nari,
  Sémi no koë. – Baijaku

(Even the camphor-tree seems to quake with the clamour of sémi!)

Sometimes the sound is compared to the noise of boiling water:—

Hizakari wa
 Niétatsu sémi no
  Hayashi kana!

(In the hour of heaviest heat, how simmers the forest with sémi!)

Niété iru
  Mizu bakari nari—
    Sémi no koë. – Taimu

(Simmers all the air with sibilation of sémi, Ceaseless, wearying sense,—a sound of perpetual boiling.)

Other poets complain especially of the multitude of the noise-makers and the ubiquity of the noise:—

Aritaké no
  Ki ni hibiki-kéri
    Sémi no koë. – Senga

(Alone I walked for miles into the wood of pine-trees: Always the one same sémi shrilled its call in my ears.)

Occasionally the subject is treated with comic exaggeration:—

Naité iru
  Ki yori mo futoshi
    Sémi no koë.

(High though the cedar be, the voice of the sémi is incomparably higher!)

Koë nagaki
  Sémi wa mijikaki
    Inochi kana!

Sémi

(How long, alas! The voice and how short the life of the sémi!)

Some poets celebrate the negative form of pleasure following upon the cessation of the sound:—

Sémi ni dété,
  Hotaru ni modoru,—
    Suzumi kana! – Yayū

(When the sémi cease their noise, and the fireflies come out—oh! how refreshing the hour!)

Sémi no tatsu,
  Ato suzushisa yo!
    Matsu no koë. – Baijaku

(When the sémi cease their storm, oh, how refreshing the stillness! Gratefully then resounds the musical speech of the pines.)

Here I may mention, by the way, that there is a little Japanese song about the *matsu no koē*, in which the onomatope "zazanza" very well represents the deep humming of the wind in the pine-needles:—

  Zazanza!
Hama-matsu no oto wa,—
  Zazanza,
  Zazanza!

(Zazanza! The sound of the pines of the shore,— Zazanza, Zazanza!)

Insect Literature

There are poets, however, who declare that the feeling produced by the noise of sémi depends altogether upon the nervous condition of the listener:—

Mori no sémi
  Suzushiki koë ya,
    Atsuki koë. – Otsushū

(Sometimes sultry the sound; sometimes, again, refreshing: The chant of the forest-sémi accords with the hearer's mood.)

Suzushisa mo
Atsusa mo sémi no
Tokoro kana! – Fuhaku

(Sometimes we think it cool,—the resting-place of the sémi, sometimes we think it hot [it is all a matter of fancy.])

Sozushii to
  Omoéba, suzushi
    Sémi no koë. – Ginkō

(If we think it is cool, then the voice of the sémi is cool [that is, the fancy changes the feeling.])

In view of the many complaints of Japanese poets about the noisiness of sémi, the reader may be surprised to learn that out of sémi-skins there used to be made in both China and Japan—perhaps upon homeopathic principles—a medicine for the cure of ear-ache!

One poem, nevertheless, proves that sémi music has its admirers:—

Sémi

O moshiroi zo ya,
Waga-ko no koë wa
Takai mori-ki no
  Sémi no koë!

(Sweet to the ear is the voice of one's own child as the voice of a sémi perched on a tall forest tree.)

But such admiration is rare. More frequently the sémi is represented as crying for its nightly repast of dew:—

Sémi wo kiké,—
  Ichi-nichi naité
    Yoru no tsuyu. – Kikaku

(Hear the sémi shrill! So, from earliest dawning, All the summer day he cries for the dew of night.)

Yū-tsuyu no
  Kuchi ni iru madé
    Naku sémi ka? – Baishitsu

(Will the sémi continue to cry till the night-dew fills its mouth?)

Occasionally the sémi is mentioned in love-songs of which the following is a fair specimen. It belongs to that class of ditties commonly sung by *geisha*. Merely as a conceit, I think it pretty, in spite of the factitious pathos; but to Japanese taste it is decidedly vulgar. The allusion to beating implies jealousy:—

Nushi ni tatakaré,
Washa matsu no sémi

Sugaritsuki-tsuki
  Naku bakari!

(Beaten by my jealous lover,—Like the sémi on the pine-tree, I can only cry and cling!)

And indeed the following tiny picture is a truer bit of work, according to Japanese art-principles (I do not know the author's name):—

Sémi hitotsu
  Matsu no yū-hi wo
    Kakaé-kéri.

(Lo! on the topmost pine, a solitary cicada; Vainly attempts to clasp one last red beam of sun.)

IV.

Philosophical verses do not form a numerous class of Japanese poems upon sémi; but they possess an interest altogether exotic. As the metamorphosis of the butterfly supplied to old Greek thought an emblem of the soul's ascension, so the natural history of the cicada has furnished Buddhism with similitudes and parables for the teaching of doctrine.

Man sheds his body only as the sémi sheds its skin. But each reincarnation obscures the memory of the previous one: we remember our former existence no more than the sémi remembers the shell from which it has emerged. Often a sémi may be found in the act of singing beside its cast-off skin; therefore a poet has written:—

Sémi

Waré to waga
  Kara ya tomurō—
    Sémi no koë. – Yayū

(Methinks that sémi sits and sings by his former body,—
Chanting the funeral service over his own dead self.)

This cast-off skin, or simulacrum,—clinging to bole or branch as in life, and seeming still to stare with great glazed eyes,—has suggested many things both to profane and to religious poets. In love-songs it is often likened to a body consumed by passionate longing. In Buddhist poetry it becomes a symbol of earthly pomp,—the hollow show of human greatness:—

Yo no naka yo
  Kaëru no hadaka,
    Sémi no kinu!

(Naked as frogs and weak we enter this life of trouble; Shedding our pomps we pass: so sémi quit their skins.)

But sometimes the poet compares the winged and shrilling sémi to a human ghost, and the broken shell to the body left behind:—

Tamashii wa
  Ukiyo ni naité,
    Sémi no kara.

(Here the forsaken shell: above me the voice of the creature; Shrills like the cry of a Soul quitting this world of pain.)

Then the great sun-quickened tumult of the cicadae—landstorm of summer life foredoomed so soon to pass away—is likened by preacher and poet to the tumult of human desire. Even as the sémi rise from earth, and climb to warmth and light, and clamour, and presently again return to dust and silence,—so rise and clamour and pass the generations of men:—

Yagaté shinu
  Keshiki wa miézu,
    Sémi no koë. – Bashō

(Never an intimation in all those voices of sémi;
How quickly the hush will come,—how speedily all must die.)

I wonder whether the thought in this little verse does not interpret something of that summer melancholy which comes to us out of nature's solitudes with the plaint of insect-voices. Unconsciously those millions of millions of tiny beings are preaching the ancient wisdom of the East,—the perpetual Sûtra of Impermanency.

Yet how few of our modern poets have given heed to the voices of insects!

Perhaps it is only to minds inexorably haunted by the Riddle of Life that Nature can speak today, in those thin sweet trillings, as she spake of old to Solomon.

The Wisdom of the East hears all things. And he that obtains it will hear the speech of insects,—as Sigurd, tasting the Dragon's Heart, heard suddenly the talking of birds.

Sémi

Notes

[1] The curious markings on the head of one variety of Japanese sémi are believed to be characters which are names of souls.

[2] In this and other citations from the Greek anthology, I have depended upon Burges's translation.

[3] That is to say, upon the sixteenth day of the seventh month.

[4] This sémi appears to be chiefly known in Shikoku.

[5] Speaking of his own attempt to make a drawing of the interior, he observes: *"Il manque à ce logis dessiné son air frêle et sa sonorité de violon sec. Dans les traits de crayon qui représentent les boiseries, il n'y a pas la precision minutieuse avec laquelle elles sont ouvragées, ni leur antiquité extrême, ni leur propreté parfaite, ni les vibrations de cigales qu'elles semblent avoir emmagasinées pendant des centaines d'été dans leurs fibres desséchées."*

[6] Japanese artists have found many a charming inspiration in the spectacle of bamboos bending under the weight of snow clinging to their tops.

[7] There is another version of this poem:—

*Omoshiroi zo ya,
Waga-ko no naku wa
Sembu-ségaki no
    Kyō yori mo!*

"More sweetly sounds the crying of one's own child than even the chanting of the *sūtra* in the service for the dead." The Buddhist service alluded to is held to be particularly beautiful.

蟲の伶人
Insect-Musicians

Mushi yo mushi,
Naïté ingwa ga
Tsukuru nara?

"O insect, insect!—think you that Karma
can be exhausted by song?" – *Japanese poem*

I.

If you ever visit Japan, be sure to go to at least one temple-festival,— *en-nichi*. The festival ought to be seen at night, when everything shows to the best advantage in the glow of countless lamps and lanterns. Until you have had this experience, you cannot know what Japan is,—you cannot imagine the real charm of queerness and prettiness, the wonderful blending of grotesquery and beauty, to be found in the life of the common people.

In such a night you will probably let yourself drift awhile with the stream of sight-seers through dazzling lanes of booths full of toys indescribable—dainty puerilities, fragile astonishments, laughter-making oddities;— you will observe representations of demons, gods, and goblins;—you will be startled by *mandō*—immense lantern-transparencies, with monstrous faces painted upon

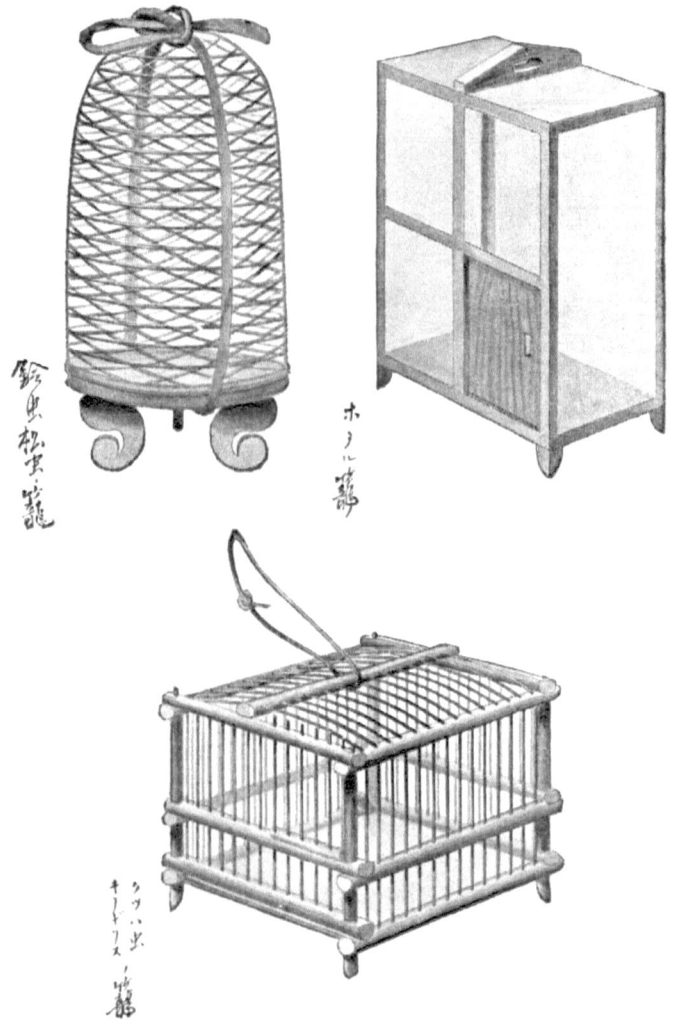

them;—you will have glimpses of jugglers, acrobats, sword-dancers, fortune-tellers;—you will hear everywhere, above the tumult of voices, a ceaseless blowing of flutes and booming of drums. All this may not be worth stopping for. But presently, I am almost sure, you will pause in your promenade to look at a booth illuminated like a magic-lantern, and stocked with tiny wooden cages out of which an incomparable shrilling proceeds. The booth is the booth of a vendor of singing-insects; and the storm of noise is made by the insects. The sight is curious; and a foreigner is nearly always attracted by it.

But having satisfied his momentary curiosity, the foreigner usually goes on his way with the idea that he has been inspecting nothing more remarkable than a particular variety of toys for children. He might easily be made to understand that the insect-trade of Tōkyō alone represents a yearly value of thousands of dollars; but he would certainly wonder if assured that the insects themselves are esteemed for the peculiar character of the sounds which they make. It would not be easy to convince him that in the aesthetic life of a most refined and artistic people, these insects hold a place not less important or well-deserved than that occupied in Western civilisation by our thrushes, linnets, nightingales, and canaries. What stranger could suppose that a literature one thousand years old,—a literature full of curious and delicate beauty,—exists upon the subject of these short-lived insect-pets?

The object of the present paper is, by elucidating these facts, to show how superficially our travellers might unconsciously judge the most interesting details of Japanese life. But such misjudgments are as natural as they are inevitable. Even with the kindest of intentions it is impossible to estimate correctly at sight anything of the extraordinary in Japanese custom, because the extraordinary nearly always relates to feelings, beliefs, or thoughts about which a stranger cannot know anything.

Before proceeding further, let me observe that the domestic insects of which I am going to speak, are mostly night-singers, and must not be confounded with the sémi (cicadae), mentioned in former essays of mine. I think that the cicadae,—even in a country so exceptionally rich as is Japan in musical insects,—are wonderful melodists in their own way. But the Japanese find as much difference between the notes of night-insects and of cicadae as we find between those of larks and sparrows; and they relegate their cicadae to the vulgar place of chatterers.

Sémi are therefore never caged. The rational liking for caged insects does not mean a liking for mere noise; and the note of every insect in public favour must possess either some rhythmic charm, or some mimetic quality celebrated in poetry or legend. The same fact is true of the Japanese liking for the chant of frogs. It would be a mistake to suppose that all kinds of frogs are considered musical; but there are particular species of very small frogs having sweet notes; and these are caged and petted.

Of course, in the proper meaning of the word, insects do not *sing*; but in the following pages I may occasionally employ the terms "singer" and "singing-insect",—partly because of their convenience, and partly because of their correspondence with the language used by Japanese insect-dealers and poets, describing the "voices", of such creatures.

II.

There are many curious references in the old Japanese classic literature to the custom of keeping musical insects. For example in the chapter entitled "Nowaki"[1] of the famous novel *Genji Monogatari*, written in the latter part of the tenth century by the Lady Murasaki-Shikibu, it is stated: "The maids were ordered to descend to the garden, and give some water to the insects." But the first definite mention of cages for singing-insects would appear to be the following passage from a work entitled *Chomon-shū*:—"On the twelfth day of the eighth month of the second year of Kaho (1,095 A. D.), the Emperor ordered his pages and chamberlains to go to Sagano and find some insects. The Emperor gave them a cage of network of bright purple thread. All, even the head-chaplain and his attendants, taking horses from the Right and the Left Imperial Mews, then went on horseback to hunt for insects. Tokinori Ben, at that time holding the office of *Kurando*,[2] proposed to the party as they rode toward Sagano, a subject for poetical composition. The subject was, *Looking for insects in the fields*. On reaching Sagano, the party dismounted, and walked in various directions for a distance of something more than ten *chō*[3] and sent their attendants to catch the insects. In the evening they returned to the palace. They put into the cage some *hagi*[4] and *ominameshi* (for the insects). The cage was respectfully presented to the Empress. There was sake-drinking in the palace that evening; and many poems were composed. The Empress and her court-ladies joined in the making of the poems."

This would appear to be the oldest Japanese record of an insect-hunt,—though the amusement may have been invented earlier than the period of Kaho. By the seventeenth century it seems to have become a popular diversion; and night-hunts were in vogue as much as day-hunts.

In the *Teikoku Bunshū*, or collected works of the poet Teikoku, who died during the second year of Shōwō (1653), there has been preserved one of the poet's letters which contains a very interesting passage on the subject. "Let us go insect-hunting this evening,"—writes the poet to his friend. "It is true that the night will be very dark, since there is no moon; and it may seem dangerous to go out. But there are many people now going to the graveyards every night, because the Bon festival is approaching[5];—therefore the way to the fields will not be lonesome for us. I have prepared many lanterns;—so the *hata-ori, matsu-mushi*, and other insects will probably come to the lanterns in great number."

It would also seem that the trade of insect-seller (*mushiya*) existed in the seventeenth century; for in a diary of that time, known as the Diary of Kikaku, the writer speaks of his disappointment at not finding any insect-dealers in Yedo,—tolerably good evidence that he had met such persons elsewhere. "On the thirteenth day of the sixth month of the fourth year of Teikyo (1687), I went out," he writes, "to look for *kirigirisu*-sellers. I searched for them in Yotsuya, in Kōjimachi, in Hongō, in Yushimasa, and in both divisions of Kanda-Sudamachō[6]; but I found none."

As we shall presently see, the *kirigirisu* was not sold in Tōkyō until about one hundred and twenty years later.

But long before it became the fashion to keep singing-insects, their music had been celebrated by poets as one of the aesthetic pleasures of the autumn. There are charming references to singing-insects in poetical collections made during the tenth century, and doubtless containing many compositions of a yet earlier period. And just as places famous for cherry, plum, or other blossoming trees, are still regularly visited every year by thousands and tens of thousands, merely for the delight of seeing the flowers in their seasons,—so in ancient times city-dwellers made autumn excursions to country-districts simply for the pleasure of hearing the chirruping choruses of crickets and of locusts,—the night-singers especially. Centuries ago places were noted as pleasure-resorts solely because of this melodious attraction;—such were Musashino (now Tōkyō), Yatano in the province of Echizen, and Mano in the province of Ōmi. Somewhat later, probably, people discovered that each of the principal species of singing-insects haunted by preference some particular locality, where its peculiar chanting could be heard to the best advantage; and eventually no less than eleven places became famous throughout Japan for different kinds of insect-music.

The best places to hear the *matsumushi* were:—

1. Arashiyama, near Kyōto,
    in the province of Yamashiro;
2. Sumiyoshi, in the province of Settsu;
3. Miyagino, in the province of Mutsu.

The best places to hear the *suzumushi* were:—

4. Kagura-ga-Oka, in Yamashiro;
5. Ogura-yama, in Yamashiro;
6. Suzuka-yama, in Isé;
7. Narumi, in Owari.

The best places to hear the *kirigirisu* were:—

8. Sagano, in Yamashiro;
9. Takeda-no-Sato, in Yamashiro;
10. Tatsuta-yama, in Yamato;
11. Ono-no-Shinowara, in Ōmi.

Insect Literature

Afterwards, when the breeding and sale of singing-insects became a lucrative industry, the custom of going into the country to hear them gradually went out of fashion. But even to-day city-dwellers, when giving a party, will sometimes place cages of singing-insects among the garden shrubbery, so that the guests may enjoy not only the music of the little creatures, but also those memories or sensations of rural peace which such music evokes.

III.

The regular trade in musical insects is of comparatively modern origin. In Tōkyō its beginnings date back only to the Kwansei era (1789-1800),—at which period, however, the capital of the Shōgunate was still called Yedo.

A complete history of the business was recently placed in my hands,—a history partly compiled from old documents, and partly from traditions preserved in the families of several noted insect merchants of the present day.

The founder of the Tōkyō trade was an itinerant foodseller named Chūzō, originally from Echigo, who settled in the Kanda district of the city in the latter part of the eighteenth century. One day, while making his usual rounds, it occurred to him to capture a few of the *suzumushi*, or bell-insects, then very plentiful in the Negishi quarter, and to try the experiment of feeding them at home. They throve and made music in confinement; and several of Chūzō's neighbours, charmed by their melodious chirruping, asked to be supplied with *suzumushi* for a consideration. From this accidental beginning, the demand for *suzumushi* grew rapidly to such proportions that the foodseller at last decided to give up his former calling and to become an insect-seller.

Insect-Musicians

Chūzō only caught and sold insects: he never imagined that it would be more profitable to breed them. But the fact was presently discovered by one of his customers,— a man named Kiriyama, then in the service of the Lord Aōyama Shimodzuké-no-kami. Kiriyama had bought from Chūzō several *suzumushi*, which were kept and fed in a jar half-filled with moist clay. They died in the cold season; but during the following summer Kiriyama was agreeably surprised to find the jar newly peopled with a number of young ones, evidently born from eggs which the first prisoners had left in the clay. He fed them carefully, and soon had the pleasure, my chronicler says, of hearing them "begin to sing in small voices". Then he resolved to make some experiments; and, aided by Chūzō, who furnished the males and females, he succeeded in breeding not only *suzumushi*, but three other kinds of singing-insects also,—*kantan*, *matsumushi*, and *kutsuwamushi*. He discovered, at the same time, that, by keeping his jars in a warm room, the insects could be hatched considerably in advance of the natural season. Chūzō sold for Kiriyama these home-bred singers; and both men found the new undertaking profitable beyond expectation.

The example set by Kiriyama was imitated by a *tabiya*, or stocking-maker named Yasubei (commonly known as Tabiya Yasubei by reason of his calling), who lived in Kanda-ku. Yasubei likewise made careful study of the habits of singing-insects, with a view to their breeding and nourishment; and he soon found himself able to carry on a small trade in them. Up to that time the insects sold in Yedo would seem to have been kept in jars or boxes: Yasubei conceived the idea of having special cages manufactured for them. A man named Kondo, vassal to the Lord Kamei of Honjo-ku, interested himself in the matter, and made a number of pretty little cages which delighted Yasubei, and secured a large order from him. The new invention found public favour at once; and Kondo soon afterwards established the first manufactory of insect-cages.

The demand for singing-insects increased from this time so rapidly, that Chūzō soon found it impossible to supply all his would-be customers directly. He therefore decided to change his business to wholesale trade, and to sell to retail dealers only. To meet orders, he purchased largely from peasants in the suburbs and elsewhere. Many persons were employed by him; and Yasubei and others paid him a fixed annual sum for sundry rights and privileges.

Some time after this Yasubei became the first itinerant-vendor of singing-insects. He walked through the streets crying his wares; but hired a number of servants to carry the cages. Tradition says that while going his rounds he used to wear a *katabira*[7] made of a much-esteemed silk stuff called *sukiya*, together with a fine Hakata-girdle; and that this elegant way of dressing proved of much service to him in his business.

Two men, whose names have been preserved, soon entered into competition with Yasubei. The first was Yasakura Yasuzō, of Honjo-ku, by previous occupation a *sahainin*, or property agent. He prospered, and became widely known as Mushi-Yasu,—"Yasu-the-Insect-Man". His success encouraged a former fellow *sahainin*, Genbei of Uyeno, to go into the same trade. Genbei likewise found insect-selling a lucrative occupation, and earned for himself the sobriquet of Mushi-Gen, by which he is yet remembered.

His descendants in Tōkyō to-day are *amé*-manufacturers[8]; but they still carry on the hereditary insect-business during the summer and autumn months; and one of the firm was kind enough to furnish me with many of the facts recorded in this little essay.

Insect-Musicians

Chūzō, the father and founder of all this curious commerce, died without children; and sometime in the period of Bunsei (1818-1829) his business was taken over by a distant relative named Yamasaki Seīchirō. To Chūzō's business, Yamasaki joined his own,—that of a toy-merchant. About the same time a law was passed limiting the number of insect-dealers in the municipality to thirty-six. The thirty-six then formed themselves into a guild, called the Ōyama-Kō ("Ōyama Society"), having for patron the divinity Sekison-sama of the mountain Ōyama in Sagami Province.[9] But in business the association was known as the Yedo-Mushi-Kō, or Yedo Insect-Company.

It is not until after this consolidation of the trade that we hear of the *kirigirisu*,—the same musical insect which the poet Kikaku had vainly tried to buy in the city in 1687,—being sold in Yedo. One of the guild known as Mushiya Kojirō ("Kojirō the Insect-Merchant"), who did business in Honjō-Ku, returning to the city after a short visit to his native place in Kadzusa, brought back with him a number of *kirigirisu*, which he sold at a good profit. Although long famous elsewhere, these insects had never before been sold in Yedo.

"When Midzu Echizen-no-Kami," says the chronicle, "became *machi-bugyō* (or chief magistrate) of Yedo, the law limiting the number of insect-dealers to thirty-six, was abolished." Whether the guild was subsequently dissolved the chronicle fails to mention.

Kiriyama, the first to breed singing-insects artificially, had, like Chūzō, built up a prosperous trade. He left a son, Kaméjirō, who was adopted into the family of one Yumoto, living in Waséda, Ushigomé-ku. Kaméjirō brought with him to the Yumoto family the valuable secrets of his father's occupation; and the Yumoto family is still celebrated in the business of insect-breeding.

Insect Literature

To-day the greatest insect-merchant in Tōkyō is said to be Kawasumi Kanésburō, of Samonchō in Yotsuya-ku. A majority of the lesser dealers obtain their autumn stock from him. But the insects bred artificially, and sold in summer, are mostly furnished by the Yumoto house. Other noted dealers are Mushi-Sei, of Shitaya-ku; and Mushi-Toku, of Asakusa. These buy insects caught in the country, and brought to the city by the peasants. The wholesale dealers supply both insects and cages to multitudes of itinerant vendors who do business in the neighbourhood of the parish temples during the *en-nichi*, or religious festivals,—especially after dark. Almost every night of the year there are *en-nichi* in some quarter of the capital; and the insect-sellers are rarely idle during the summer and autumn months.

Perhaps the following list of current Tōkyō prices[10] for singing-insects may interest the reader:—

>   *Suzumushi* . . . . 3 sen 5 rin, to 4 sen
>   *Matsumushi* . . . . 4 " . . . . 5 "
>   *Kantan*. . . . . 10 " . . . . 12 "
>   *Kin-hibari* . . . . 10 " . . . . 12 "
>   *Kusa-hibari*. . . . . . . 10 " . . . . 12 "
>   *Kuro-hibari* . . . . 8 " . . . . 12 "
>   *Kutsuwamushi* . . . . 10 " . . . . 15 "
>   *Yamato-suzu*. . . . . . . 8 " . . . . 12 "
>   *Kirigirisu* . . . . 12 " . . . . 15 "
>   *Emma-kōrogi* . . . . . . 5 "
>   *Kanétataki* . . . . 12 "
>   *Umaoi* . . . . 10 "

These prices, however, rule only during the busy period of the insect trade. In May and the latter part of June the prices are high,—for only artificially bred insects are then in the market. In July *kirigirisu* brought from the country will sell as low as one *sen*. The *kantan*, *kusa-hibari*, and *Yamato-suzu* sell sometimes as low as two *sen*. In August the *Emma-kōrogi* can be bought even at the rate of ten for one *sen*; and in September the *kuro-hibari*, *kanétataki*, and *umaoi* sell for one or one and a half *sen* each. But there is little variation at any season in the prices of *suzumushi* and of *matsumushi*. These are never very dear, but never sell at less than three *sen*; and there is always a demand for them. The *suzumushi* is the most popular of all; and the greater part of the profits annually made in the insect-trade is said to be gained on the sale of this insect.

IV.

As will be seen from the foregoing price-list, twelve varieties of musical insects are sold in Tōkyō. Nine can be artificially bred,—namely the *suzumushi, matsumushi, kirigirisu, kantan, kutsuwamushi, Emma-kōrogi, kin-hibari, kusa-hibari* (also called *Asa-suzu*), and the *Yamato-suzu*, or *Yoshino-suzu*. Three varieties, I am told, are not bred for sale, but captured for the market: these are the *kanétataki, umaoi* or *hataori*, and *kuro-hibari*. But a considerable number of all the insects annually offered for sale, are caught in their native haunts.

The night-singers are, with few exceptions, easily taken. They are captured with the help of lanterns. Being quickly attracted by light, they approach the lanterns; and when near enough to be observed, they can readily be covered with nets or little baskets. Males and females are usually secured at the same time, for the creatures move about in couples. Only the males sing; but a certain number of females are always taken for breeding purposes. Males and females are kept in the same vessel only for breeding: they are never left together in a cage, because the male ceases to sing when thus mated, and will die in a short time after pairing.

The breeding pairs are kept in jars or other earthen vessels half-filled with moistened clay, and are supplied every day with fresh food.

They do not live long: the male dies first, and the female survives only until her eggs have been laid. The young insects hatched from them, shed their skin in about forty days from birth, after which they grow more rapidly, and soon attain their full development. In their natural state these creatures are hatched a little before the Doyō, or Period of Greatest Heat by the old calendar,—that is to say, about the middle of July;—and they begin to sing in October.

But when bred in a warm room, they are hatched early in April; and, with careful feeding, they can be offered for sale before the end of May.

When very young, their food is triturated and spread for them upon a smooth piece of wood; but the adults are usually furnished with unprepared food,—consisting of parings of egg-plant, melon-rind, cucumber-rind, or the soft interior parts of the white onion. Some insects, however, are specially nourished;—the *abura-kirigirisu*, for example, being fed with sugar-water and slices of musk-melon.

V.

All the insects mentioned in the Tōkyō price-list are not of equal interest; and several of the names appear to refer only to different varieties of one species,—though on this point I am not positive. Some of the insects do not seem to have yet been scientifically classed; and I am no entomologist. But I can offer some general notes on the more important among the little melodists, and free translations of a few out of the countless poems about them,—beginning with the *matsumushi*, which was celebrated in Japanese verse a thousand years ago:

Matsumushi.[11]

As ideographically written, the name of this creature signifies "pine-insect"; but, as pronounced, it might mean also "waiting-insect", since the verb "*matsu*", "to wait", and the noun "*matsu*", "pine", have the same sound. It is chiefly upon this double meaning of the word as uttered that a host of Japanese poems about the *matsumushi* are based. Some of these are very old,—dating back to the tenth century at least.

Although by no means a rare insect, the *matsumushi* is much esteemed for the peculiar clearness and sweetness of its notes—(onomatopoetically rendered in Japanese by the syllables *chin-chirorīn, chin-chirorīn*),—little silvery shrillings which I can best describe as resembling the sound of an electric bell heard from a distance. The *matsumushi* haunts pine-woods and cryptomeria-groves, and makes its music at night. It is a very small insect, with a dark-brown back, and a yellowish belly.

Perhaps the oldest extant verses upon the *matsumushi* are those contained in the *Kokinshū*,—a famous anthology compiled in the year 905 by the court-poet Tsurayuki and several of his noble friends. Here we first find that play on the name of the insect as pronounced, which was to be repeated in a thousand different keys by a multitude of poets through the literature of more than nine hundred years:—

Aki no no ni
Michi mo madoinu;

Insect Literature

> *Matsumushi no*
> *Koe suru kata ni*
> *Yadoya karamashi.*

"In the autumn-fields I lose my way;—perhaps I might ask for lodging in the direction of the cry of the waiting-insect";—that is to say, "might sleep to-night in the grass where the insects are waiting for me." There is in the same work a much prettier poem on the *matsumushi* by Tsurayuki.

> *With dusk begins to cry the male of the Waiting-insect;—*
> *I too, await my beloved, and, hearing, my longing grows.*

The following poems on the same insect are less ancient but not less interesting:—

> *Forever past and gone, the hour of the promised advent!*
> *Truly the Waiter's voice is a voice of sadness now!*

> *Parting is sorrowful always,—even the parting with*
>   *autumn!*
> *O plaintive matsumushi, add not thou to my pain!*

> *Always more clear and shrill, as the hush of the night*
>   *grows deeper,*
> *The Waiting-insect's voice;—and I that wait in the garden,*
> *Feel enter into my heart the voice and the moon together.*

Suzumushi.[12]

The name signifies "bell-insect"; but the bell of which the sound is thus referred to is a very small bell, or a bunch of little bells such as a Shinto priestess uses in the sacred dances. The *suzumushi* is a great favourite with insect-fanciers, and is bred in great numbers for the market. In the wild state it is found in many parts of Japan; and at night the noise made by multitudes of *suzumushi* in certain lonesome places might easily be mistaken,—as it has been by myself more than once,—for the sound of rapids. The Japanese description of the insect as resembling "a watermelon seed"—the black kind—is excellent. It is very small, with a black back, and a white or yellowish belly. Its tintinnabulation—*ri-i-i-i-in*, as the Japanese render the sound—might easily be mistaken for the tinkling of a *suzu*. Both the *matsumushi* and the *suzumushi* are mentioned in Japanese poems of the period of Engi (901-922).

Some of the following poems on the *suzumushi* are very old; others are of comparatively recent date:—

Yes, my dwelling is old: weeds on the roof are growing;—
But the voice of the suzumushi—that will never be old!

To-day united in love,—we who can meet so rarely!
Hear how the insects ring!—their bells to our hearts
    keep time.

The tinkle of tiny bells,—the voices of suzumushi,
I hear in the autumn-dusk,—and think of the fields at home.

Even the moonshine sleeps on the dews of the garden-grasses;
Nothing moves in the night but the suzumushi's voice.

Heard in these alien fields, the voice of the suzumushi,—
Sweet in the evening-dusk,—sounds like the sound of home.

Vainly the suzumushi exhausts its powers of pleasing,
Always, the long night through, my tears continue to flow!

Insect Literature

*Hark to those tinkling tones,—the chant of the suzumushi!
—If a jewel of dew could sing, it would tinkle with such
a voice!*

*Foolish-fond I have grown;—I feel for the suzumushi!—
In the time of the heavy rains, what will the creature do?*

Hataori-mushi.

The *hataori* is a beautiful bright-green grasshopper, of very graceful shape. Two reasons are given for its curious name, which signifies "the Weaver". One is that, when held in a particular way, the struggling gestures of the creature resemble the movements of a girl weaving. The other reason is that its music seems to imitate the sound of the reed and shuttle of a hand-loom in operation,—*ji-ī-ī-ī-chon-chon!—ji-ī-ī-ī-chon-chon!*

There is a pretty folk-story about the origin of the *hataori* and the *kirigirisu*, which used to be told to Japanese children in former times. Long, long ago, says the tale, there were two very dutiful daughters who supported their old blind father by the labour of their hands. The elder girl used to weave, and the younger to sew. When the old blind father died at last, these good girls grieved so much that they soon died also. One beautiful morning, some creatures of a kind never seen before were found making music above the graves of the sisters. On the tomb of the elder was a pretty green insect, producing sounds like those made by a girl weaving, *ji-ī-ī-ī, chon-chon! ji-ī-ī-ī, chon-chon!* This was the first *hataori-mushi*. On the tomb of the younger sister was an insect which kept crying out, "*Tsuzuré-sasé, sasé, sasé!—tsuzuré, tsuzuré—sasé, sasé, sasé!*" (Torn clothes—patch, patch them up!—torn clothes, torn clothes—patch up, patch up, patch up!) This was the first *kirigirisu*. Then everybody knew that the spirits of the good sisters had taken those shapes. Still every autumn they cry to wives and daughters to work well at the loom, and warn them to repair the winter garments of the household before the coming of the cold.

Such poems as I have been able to obtain about the *hataori* consist of nothing more than pretty fancies. Two, of which I offer free renderings, are ancient,—the first by Tsurayuki; the second by a poetess classically known as "Akinaka's Daughter":—

Weaving-insects I hear; and the fields, in their autumn colours,
Seem of Chinese-brocade:—was this the weavers' work?

Gossamer-threads are spread over the shrubs and grasses:
Weaving-insects I hear;—do they weave with spider-silk?

Umaoi.

The *umaoi* is sometimes confounded with the *hataori*, which it much resembles. But the true *umaoi*—(called *junta* in Izumo)—is a shorter and thicker insect than the *hataori*; and has at its tail a hook-shaped protuberance, which the weaver-insect has not. Moreover, there is some difference in the sounds made by the two creatures. The music of the *umaoi* is not "*ji-ī-ī-ī,—chon-chon*", but, "*zu-ī-in-tzō!—zu-ī-in-tzō!*"—say the Japanese.

Kirigirisu.[13]

There are different varieties of this much-prized insect. The *abura-kirigirisu*, a day-singer, is a delicate creature, and must be carefully nourished in confinement. The *tachi-kirigirisu*, a night-singer, is more commonly found in the market.

Captured *kirigirisu* sold in Tōkyō are mostly from the neighbourhood of Itabashi, Niiso, and Todogawa; and these, which fetch high prices, are considered the best. They are large vigorous insects, uttering very clear notes. From Kujiukuri in Kadzusa other and much cheaper *kirigirisu* are brought to the capital; but these have a disagreeable odour, suffer from the attacks of a peculiar parasite, and are feeble musicians.

As stated elsewhere, the sounds made by the *kirigirisu* are said to resemble those of the Japanese words, "*Tsuzuré—sasé! sasé!*" (Torn clothes—patch up! patch up!); and a large proportion of the many poems written about the insect depend for interest upon ingenious but untranslatable allusions to those words. I offer renderings therefore of only two poems on the *kirigirisu*,—the first by an unknown poet in the Kokinshū; the second by Tadafusa:—

> *O Kirigirisu! when the clover changes colour,*
> *Are the nights then sad for you as for me that cannot sleep?*

> *O Kirigirisu! cry not, I pray, so loudly!*
> *Hearing, my sorrow grows,—and the autumn-night is long!*

The *kusa-hibari*, or "Grass-Lark",—also called *Asa-suzu*, or "Morning-Bell"; *Yabu-suzu*, or "the Little Bell of the Bamboogrove"; *Aki-kazé*, or "Autumn-Wind"; and *Ko-suzu-mushi*, or "the Child of the Bell-Insect",—is a day-singer. It is very small,—perhaps the smallest of the insect choir, except the *Yamato-suzu*.

Kin-hibari.

The *kin-hibari*, or "Golden Lark", used to be found in great numbers about the neighbourhood of the well-known *Shinobazu-no-iké*,—the great lotus-pond of Uyeno in Tōkyō;—but of late years it has become scarce there. The *kin-hibari* now sold in the capital are brought from Todogawa and Shimura.

Kuro-hibari.

The *kuro-hibari*, or "Black Lark", is rather uncommon, and comparatively dear. It is caught in the country about Tōkyō, but is never bred.

Kōrogi.

There are many varieties of this night-cricket,—called *kōrogi* from its music:—"*kiri-kiri-kiri-kiri!—kōro-kōro-kōro-kōro!-ghi-ī-ī-ī-ī-ī!*" One variety, the *ebi-kōrogi*, or "shrimp kōrogi", does not make any sound. But the *uma-kōrogi*, or "horse-kōrogi"; the *Oni-kōrogi*, or "Demon-kōrogi"; and the *Emma-kōrogi*, or "Cricket-of-Emma[14] (King of the Dead)", are all good musicians. The colour is blackish-brown, or black;—the best singing-varieties have curious wavy markings on the wings.

An interesting fact regarding the *kōrogi* is that mention of it is made in the very oldest collection of Japanese poems known,—the *Manyōshu*, probably compiled about the middle of the eighth century. The following lines, by an unknown poet, which contain this mention, are therefore considerably more than eleven hundred years old:—

Niwa-kusa ni
Murasamé furité
  Kōrogi no
Naku oto kikeba
  Aki tsukinikeri.

("Showers have sprinkled the garden-grass. Hearing the sound of the crying of the *Kōrogi*, I know that the autumn has come.")

Kutsuwamushi.

There are several varieties of this extraordinary creature,—also called onomatopoetically *gatcha-gatcha*,—which is most provokingly described in dictionaries as "a kind of noisy cricket"! The variety commonly sold in Tōkyō has a green back, and a yellowish-white abdomen; but there are also brown and reddish varieties. The *kutsuwamushi* is difficult to capture, but easy to breed. As the *tsuku-tsuku-bōshi* is the most wonderful musician among the sun-loving cicadæ or *sémi*, so the *kutsuwamushi* is the most wonderful of night-crickets. It owes its name, which means "The Bridle-bit-Insect", to its noise, which resembles the jingling and ringing of the old fashioned Japanese bridle-bit (*kutsuwa*). But the sound is really much louder and much more complicated than ever was the jingling of a single *kutsuwa*; and the accuracy of the comparison is not easily discerned while the creature is storming beside you. Without the evidence of one's own eyes, it were hard to believe that so small a life could make so prodigious a noise. Certainly the vibratory apparatus in this insect must be very complicated. The sound begins with a thin sharp whizzing, as of leaking steam, and slowly strengthens;—then to the whizzing is suddenly added a quick dry clatter, as of castanets;—and then, as the whole machinery rushes into operation, you hear, high above the whizzing and the clatter, a torrent of rapid ringing tones like the tapping of a gong. These, the last to begin, are also the first to cease; then the castanets stop; and finally the whizzing dies;—but the full orchestra may remain in operation for several hours at a time, without a pause. Heard from far

Insect-Musicians

away at night the sound is pleasant, and is really so much like the ringing of a bridle-bit, that when you first listen to it you cannot but feel how much real poetry belongs to the name of this insect,—celebrated from of old as "playing at ghostly escort in ways where no man can pass".

The most ancient poem on the *kutsuwamushi* is perhaps the following, by the Lady Idzumi Shikibu:—

Waga seko wa
Koma ni makasété
 Kinikeri to,
Kiku ni kikasuru
 Kutsuwamushi kana!

—which might be thus freely rendered:

Listen!—his bridle rings;—that is surely my husband
Homeward hurrying now—fast as the horse can bear him!
Ah! my ear was deceived!—only the Kutsuwamushi!

Kantan.

This insect—also called *kantan-gisu*, and *kantan-no-kirigirisu*,—is a dark-brown night-cricket. Its note—"*zi-ī-ī-in*"—is peculiar. I can only compare it to the prolonged twang of a bow-string. But this comparison is not satisfactory, because there is a penetrant metallic quality in the twang, impossible to describe.

VI.

Besides poems about the chanting of particular insects, there are countless Japanese poems, ancient and modern, upon the voices of night-insects in general,—chiefly in relation to the autumn season. Out of a multitude I have selected and translated a few of the more famous only, as typical of the sentiment or fancy of hundreds. Although some of my renderings are far from literal as to language, I believe that they express with tolerable faithfulness the thought and feeling of the originals:—

Not for my sake alone, I know, is the autumn's coming;—
Yet, hearing the insects sing, at once my heart grows sad.
– Kokinshū

Faint in the moonshine sounds the chorus of insect-voices:
Tonight the sadness of autumn speaks in their plaintive tone.

I never can find repose in the chilly nights of autumn,
Because of the pain I hear in the insects' plaintive song.

How must it be in the fields where the dews are falling thickly!
In the insect-voices that reach me I hear the tingling of cold.

Never I dare to take my way through the grass in autumn:
Should I tread upon insect-voices[15]—what would my
    feelings be!

The song is ever the same, but the tones of the insects differ,
Maybe their sorrows vary, according to their hearts.
– Idzumi-Shikibu

Changed is my childhood's home—all but those insect-voices:
I think they are trying to speak of happier days that were.

These trembling dews on the grass—are they tears for the
    death of autumn?—
Tears of the insect-singers that now so sadly cry?

It might be thought that several of the poems above given were intended to express either a real or an affected sympathy with imagined insect pain. But this would be a wrong interpretation. In most compositions of this class, the artistic purpose is to suggest, by indirect means, various phases of the emotion of love,—especially that melancholy which lends its own passional tone to the aspects and the voices of nature. The baroque fancy that dew might be insect-tears, is by its very exaggeration intended to indicate the extravagance of grief, as well as to suggest that human tears have been freshly shed. The verses in which a woman declares that her heart has become too affectionate, since she cannot but feel for the bell-insect during a heavy shower, really bespeak the fond anxiety felt for some absent beloved, travelling in the time of the great rains. Again, in the lines about "treading on insect-voices", the dainty scruple is uttered only as a hint of that intensification of feminine tenderness which love creates. And a still more remarkable example of this indirect double-suggestiveness is offered by the little poem prefacing this article,—

"O insect, insect!—think you that Karma can be exhausted by song?"

The Western reader would probably suppose that the insect-condition, or insect-state-of-being, is here referred to; but the real thought of the speaker, presumably a woman, is that her own sorrow is the result of faults committed in former lives, and is therefore impossible to alleviate.

It will have been observed that a majority of the verses cited refer to autumn and to the sensations of autumn. Certainly Japanese poets have not been insensible to the real melancholy inspired by autumn,—that vague strange annual revival of ancestral pain: dim inherited sorrow of millions of memories associated through millions of years with the death of summer;—but in nearly every utterance of this melancholy, the veritable allusion is to grief of parting. With its colour-changes, its leaf-whirlings, and the ghostly plaint of its insect-voices, autumn Buddhistically symbolises impermanency, the certainty of bereavement, the pain that clings to all desire, and the sadness of isolation.

But even if these poems on insects were primarily intended to shadow amorous emotion, do they not reflect also for us the subtlest influences of nature,—wild pure nature,—upon imagination and memory? Does not the place accorded to insect-melody, in the home-life as well as in the literature of Japan, prove an aesthetic sensibility developed in directions that yet remain for us almost unexplored? Does not the shrilling booth of the insect-seller at a night-festival proclaim even a popular and universal comprehension of things divined in the West only by our rarest poets:—the pleasure-pain of autumn's beauty, the weird sweetness of the voices of the night, the magical quickening of remembrance by echoes of forest and field? Surely we have something to learn from the people in whose mind the simple chant of a cricket can awaken whole fairy—swarms of tender and delicate fancies. We may boast of being their masters in the mechanical,—their teachers of the artificial in all its varieties of ugliness;—but in the knowledge of the natural,—in the feeling of the joy and beauty of earth,—they exceed us like the Greeks of old. Yet perhaps it will be only when our blind aggressive industrialism has wasted and sterilised their paradise,—substituting everywhere for beauty the utilitarian, the conventional, the vulgar, the utterly hideous,—that we shall begin with remorseful amazement to comprehend the charm of that which we destroyed.

Insect-Musicians

Notes

[1] *Nowaki* is the name given to certain destructive storms usually occurring toward the end of autumn. All the chapters of the *Genji Monogatari* have remarkably poetical and effective titles. There is an English translation by Mr. Kenchō Suyematsu, of the first seventeen chapters.

[2] The *Kurando*, or *Kurōdo*, was an official entrusted with the care of the imperial records.

[3] A *chō* is about one-fifteenth of a mile.

[4] *Hagi* is the name commonly given to the bush-clover. *Ominameshi* is the common term for the *Valeriana officinalis*.

[5] That is to say, there are now many people who go every night to the graveyards, to decorate and prepare the graves before the great Festival of the Dead.

[6] Most of those names survive in the appellations of well-known districts of the present Tōkyō.

[7] *Katabira* is a name given to many kinds of light textures used for summer-robes. The material is usually hemp, but sometimes, as in the case referred to here, of fine silk. Some of these robes are transparent, and very beautiful.—Hakata, in Kyūshū, is still famous for the silk girdles made there. The fabric is very heavy and strong.

[8] *Amé* is a nutritive gelatinous extract obtained from wheat and other substances. It is sold in many forms—as candy, as a syrupy liquid resembling molasses, as a sweet hot

drink, as a solid jelly. Children are very fond of it. Its principal element is starch-sugar.

[9] Ōyama Mountain in Sagami is a great resort of Pilgrims. There is a celebrated temple there, dedicated to Iwanaga-Himé ("Long-Rock Princess"), sister of the beautiful Goddess of Fuji. Sekison-san is a popular name both for the divinity and for the mountain itself.

[10] Prices of the year 1897.

[11] *Calyptotryphus marmoratus?*

[12] *Homeogryllus japonicus.*

[13] *Locusta japonica?*

[14] Sanscrit: *Yama.* Probably this name was given to the insect on account of its large staring eyes. Images of King Emma are always made with very big and awful eyes.

[15] *Mushi no koe fumu.*

草雲雀
Kusa-Hibari

"Issun no mushi ni mo gobu no tamashii."
– *Japanese proverb*

His cage is exactly two Japanese inches high and one inch and a half wide: its tiny wooden door, turning upon a pivot, will scarcely admit the tip of my little finger. But he has plenty of room in that cage,—room to walk, and jump, and fly; for he is so small that you must look very carefully through the brown-gauze sides of it in order to catch a glimpse of him. I have always to turn the cage round and round, several times, in a good light, before I can discover his whereabouts; and then I usually find him resting in one of the upper corners,—clinging, upside down, to his ceiling of gauze.

Imagine a cricket about the size of an ordinary mosquito,—with a pair of antennae much longer than his own body, and so fine that you can distinguish them only against the light. *Kusa-hibari*, or "Grass-Lark", is the Japanese name of him; and he is worth in the market exactly twelve cents: that is to say, very much more than his weight in gold. Twelve cents for such a gnat-like thing! . . .

By day he sleeps or meditates, except while occupied with the slice of fresh egg-plant or cucumber which must be poked into his cage every morning . . . To keep him clean and well fed is somewhat troublesome: could you see

Kusa-Hibari

him, you would think it absurd to take any pains for the sake of a creature so ridiculously small.

But always at sunset the infinitesimal soul of him awakens: then the room begins to fill with a delicate and ghostly music of indescribable sweetness,—a thin, thin silvery rippling and trilling as of tiniest electric bells. As the darkness deepens, the sound becomes sweeter,—sometimes swelling till the whole house seems to vibrate with the elfish resonance,—sometimes thinning down into the faintest imaginable thread of a voice. But loud or low, it keeps a penetrating quality that is weird . . . All night the atomy thus sings: he ceases only when the temple bell proclaims the hour of dawn.

Now this tiny song is a song of love,—vague love of the unseen and unknown. It is quite impossible that he should ever have seen or known, in this present existence of his. Not even his ancestors, for many generations back, could have known anything of the night-life of the fields, or the amorous value of song. They were born of eggs hatched in a jar of clay, in the shop of some insect-merchant; and they dwelt thereafter only in cages. But he sings the song of his race as it was sung a myriad years ago, and as faultlessly as if he understood the exact significance of every note. Of course he did not learn the song. It is a song of organic memory,—deep, dim memory of other quintillions of lives, when the ghost of him shrilled at night from the dewy grasses of the hills. Then that song brought him love,—and death. He has forgotten all about death; but he remembers the love. And therefore he sings now,—for the bride that will never come.

So that his longing is unconsciously retrospective: he cries to the dust of the past,—he calls to the silence and the gods for the return of time . . . Human lovers do very much the same thing without knowing it. They call their illusion an Ideal; and their Ideal is, after all, a mere shadowing of race-experience, a phantom of organic memory. The living present has very little to do with it . . . Perhaps this atomy also has an ideal, or at least the rudiment of an ideal; but, in any event, the tiny desire must utter its plaint in vain.

The fault is not altogether mine. I had been warned that if the creature were mated, he would cease to sing and would speedily die. But, night after night, the plaintive, sweet, unanswered trilling touched me like a reproach,—became at last an obsession, an affliction, a torment of conscience; and I tried to buy a female. It was too late in the season; there were no more *kusa-hibari* for sale,—either males or females. The insect-merchant laughed and said, "He ought to have died about the twentieth day of the ninth month." (It was already the second day of the tenth month.) But the insect-merchant did not know that I have a good stove in my study, and keep the temperature at above 75° F. Wherefore my grass-lark still sings at the close of the eleventh month, and I hope to keep him alive until the Period of Greatest Cold. However, the rest of his generation are probably dead: neither for love nor money could I now find him a mate. And were I to set him free in order that he might make the search for himself, he could not possibly live through a single night, even if fortunate enough to escape by day the multitude of his natural enemies in the garden,—ants, centipedes, and ghastly earth-spiders.

Last evening,—the twenty-ninth of the eleventh month—an odd feeling came to me as I sat at my desk: a sense of emptiness in the room. Then I became aware that my grass-lark was silent, contrary to his wont. I went to the silent cage, and found him lying dead beside a dried-up lump of egg-plant as grey and hard as a stone. Evidently he had not been fed for three or four days; but only the night before his death he had been singing wonderfully,—so that I foolishly imagined him to be more than usually contented. My student, Aki, who loves insects, used to feed him; but Aki had gone into the country for a week's holiday, and the duty of caring for the grass-lark had devolved upon Hana, the housemaid. She is not sympathetic, Hana the housemaid. She says that she did not forget the mite,—but there was no more egg-plant. And she had never thought of substituting a slice of onion or of cucumber! . . . I spoke words of reproof to Hana the housemaid, and she dutifully expressed contrition. But the fairy-music has stopped; and the stillness reproaches; and the room is cold, in spite of the stove.

Absurd! . . . I have made a good girl unhappy because of an insect half the size of a barley-grain! The quenching of that infinitesimal life troubles me more than I could have believed possible . . . Of course, the mere habit of thinking about a creature's wants—even the wants of a cricket—may create, by insensible degrees, an imaginative interest, an attachment of which one becomes conscious only when the relation is broken. Besides, I had felt so much, in the hush of the night, the charm of the delicate voice,—telling of one minute existence dependent upon my will and selfish pleasure, as upon the favour of a god,—telling me also that the atom of ghost in the tiny cage, and the atom of ghost within myself, were forever but one and the same in the deeps of the Vast of being . . . And then to think of the little creature hungering and thirsting, night after night, and day after day, while the thoughts of his guardian deity were turned to the weaving of dreams! . . . How bravely, nevertheless, he sang on to the very end,—an atrocious end, for he had eaten his own legs! . . . May the gods forgive us all,—especially Hana the housemaid! Yet, after all, to devour one's own legs for hunger is not the worst that can happen to a being cursed with the gift of song. There are human crickets who must eat their own hearts in order to sing.

昆蟲を詠んだ詩
Some Poems about Insects

One of the great defects of English books printed in the last century is the want of an index. The importance of being able to refer at once to any subject treated of in a book was not recognised until the days when exact scholarship necessitated indexing of the most elaborate kind. But even now we constantly find good books severely criticised because of this deficiency. All that I have said tends to show that even to-day in Western countries the immense importance of systematic arrangement in literary collections is not sufficiently recognised. We have, of course, a great many English anthologies,—that is to say, collections of the best typical compositions of a certain epoch in poetry or in prose. But you must have observed that, in Western countries, nearly all such anthologies are compiled chronologically—not according to the subject of the poems. To this general rule there are indeed a few exceptions. There is a collection of love poetry by Watson, which is famous; a collection of child poetry by Patmore; a collection of "society verse" by Locker; and several things of that sort. But even here the arrangement is not of a special kind; nor is it ever divided according to the subject of each particular poem. I know that some books have been published of late years with such titles as "Poems of the Sea", "Poems of Nature"—but these are of no literary importance at all and they are not compiled by competent critics. Besides, the subject-heads are always of much too general a kind. The French are far in advance of the English in the art of making anthologies; but even in such splendid anthologies as those of Crépet and of Lemerre the arrangement is of the most general kind,—chronological, and little more.

I was reminded to tell you this, because of several questions recently asked me, which I found it impossible to answer. Many a Japanese student might suppose that Western poetry has its classified arrangements corresponding in some sort to those of Japanese poetry. Perhaps the Germans have something of the kind, but the English and French have not. Any authority upon the subject of Japanese literature can, I have been told, inform himself almost immediately as to all that has been written in poetry upon a particular subject. Japanese poetry has been classified and sub-classified and double-indexed or even quadruple-indexed after a manner incomparably more exact than anything English anthologies can show. I am aware that this fact is chiefly owing to the ancient rules about subjects, seasons, contrasts, and harmonies, after which the old poets used to write. But whatever be said about such rules, there can be no doubt at all of the excellence of the arrangements which the rules produced. It is greatly to be regretted that we have not in English a system of arrangement enabling the student to discover quickly all that has been written upon a particular subject—such as roses, for example, or pine trees, or doves, or the beauties of the autumn season. There is nobody to tell you where to find such things; and as the whole range of English poetry is so great that it takes a great many years even to glance through it, a memorised knowledge of the subjects is impossible for the average man. I believe that Macaulay would have been able to remember almost any

Some Poems about Insects

reference in the poetry then accessible to scholars,—just as the wonderful Greek scholar Porson could remember the exact place of any text in the whole of Greek literature, and even all the variations of that text. But such men are born only once in hundreds of years; the common memory can not attempt to emulate their feats. And it is very difficult at the present time for the ordinary student of poetry to tell you just how much has been written upon any particular subject by the best English poets.

Now you will recognise some difficulties in the way of a lecturer in attempting to make classifications of English poetry after the same manner that Japanese classification can be made of Japanese poetry. One must read enormously merely to obtain one's materials, and even then the result is not to be thought of as exhaustive. I am going to try to give you a few lectures upon English poetry thus classified, but we must not expect that the lectures will be authoritatively complete. Indeed, we have no time for lectures of so thorough a sort. All that I can attempt will be to give you an idea of the best things that English poets have thought and expressed upon certain subjects.

You know that the old Greeks wrote a great deal of beautiful poetry about insects,—especially about musical insects, crickets, cicadas, and other insects such as those the Japanese poets have been writing about for so many hundreds of years. But in modern Western poetry there is very little, comparatively speaking, about insects. The English poets have all written a great deal about birds, and especially about singing birds; but very little has been written upon the subject of insects—singing insects. One reason is probably that the number of musical insects in England is very small, perhaps owing to the climate. American poets have written more about insects than English poets have done, though their work is of a much less finished kind. But this is because musical insects in America are very numerous. On the whole, we may say that neither in English nor in French poetry will you find much about the Voices of crickets, locusts, or cicadae. I could not even give you a special lecture upon that subject. We must take the subject "insect" in a rather general signification; and if we do that we can edit together a nice little collection of poetical examples.

The butterfly was regarded by the Greeks especially as the emblem of the soul and therefore of immortality. We have several Greek remains, picturing the butterfly as perched upon a skull, thus symbolising life beyond death. And the metamorphosis of the insect is, you know, very often referred to in Greek philosophy. We might expect that English poets would have considered the butterfly especially from this point of view; and we do have a few examples. Perhaps the best known is that of Coleridge.

> The butterfly the ancient Grecians made
> The soul's fair emblem, and its only name—
> But of the soul, escaped the slavish trade
> Of earthly life! For in this mortal frame
> Ours is the reptile's lot, much toil, much blame,
> Manifold motions making little speed,
> And to deform and kill the things whereon we feed.

The allusion to the "name" is of course to the Greek word, *psyche*, which signifies both soul and butterfly. Psyche, as the soul, was pictured by the Greeks as a beautiful girl, with a somewhat sad face, and butterfly wings springing from her shoulders. Coleridge tells us here that although the Greeks likened the soul to the butterfly, we must remember what the butterfly really is,—the last and highest state of insect-being—"escaped the slavish trade of earthly life". What is this so-called slavish trade?

Some Poems about Insects

It is the necessity of working and struggling in order to live—in order to obtain food. The butterfly is not much of an eater; some varieties, indeed, do not eat at all. All the necessity for eating ended with the life of the larva. In the same manner religion teaches that the soul represents the changed state of man. In this life a man is only like a caterpillar; death changes him into a chrysalis, and out of the chrysalis issues the winged soul which does not have to trouble itself about such matters as eating and drinking. By the word "reptile" in this verse, you must understand caterpillar. Therefore the poet speaks of all our human work as manifold motions making little speed; you have seen how many motions a caterpillar must make in order to go even a little distance, and you must have noticed the manner in which it spoils the appearance of the plant upon which it feeds. There is here an allusion to the strange and terrible fact, that all life—and particularly the life of man—is maintained only by the destruction of other life. In order to live we must kill—perhaps only plants, but in any case we must kill.

Wordsworth has several poems on butterflies, but only one of them is really fine. It is fine, not because it suggests any deep problem, but because with absolute simplicity it pictures the charming difference of character in a little boy and a little girl playing together in the fields. The poem is addressed to the butterfly.

> Stay near me—do not take thy flight!
> A little longer stay in sight!
> Much converse do I find in thee,
> Historian of my infancy!
> Float near me; do not yet depart!
> Dead times revive in thee:
> Thou bring'st, gay creature as thou art!

A solemn image to my heart,
   My father's family.

Oh! pleasant, pleasant were the days,
The time, when, in our childish plays,
My sister Emmeline and I
Together chased the butterfly!
A very hunter did I rush
Upon the prey: with leaps and springs
I followed on from brake to bush;
But she, God love her, feared to brush
The dust from off its wings.

What we call and what looks like dust on the wings of a butterfly, English children are now taught to know as really beautiful scales or featherlets, but in Wordsworth's time the real structure of the insect was not so well known as now to little people. Therefore to the boy the coloured matter brushed from the wings would only have seemed so much dust. But the little girl, with the instinctive tenderness of the future mother-soul in her, dreads to touch those strangely delicate wings; she fears, not only to spoil, but also to hurt.

Deeper thoughts than memory may still be suggested to English poets by the sight of a butterfly, and probably will be for hundreds of years to come. Perhaps the best poem of a half-metaphorical, half-philosophical thought about butterflies is the beautiful prologue to Browning's "Fifine at the Fair", which prologue is curiously entitled "Amphibian"—implying that we are about to have a reference to creatures capable of living in two distinctive elements, yet absolutely belonging neither to the one nor to the other. The poet swims out far into the sea on a beautiful day; and, suddenly, looking up, perceives a beautiful butterfly flying over his head, as if watching him. The sight of the insect at once suggests to him its relation to Greek fancy as a name for the soul; then he begins to wonder whether it might not really be the soul, or be the symbol of the soul, of a dead woman who loved him. From that point of the poem begins a little metaphysical fantasy about the possible condition of souls.

> The fancy I had to-day,
> Fancy which turned a fear!
> I swam far out in the bay,
> Since waves laughed warm and clear.
>
> I lay and looked at the sun,
> The noon-sun looked at me:
> Between us two, no one
> Live creature, that I could see.
>
> Yes! There came floating by
> Me, who lay floating too,
> Such a strange butterfly!
> Creature as dear as new:
>
> Because the membraned wings
> So wonderful, so wide,
> So sun-suffused, were things
> Like soul and nought beside.

So much for the conditions of the poet's revery. He is swimming in the sea; above his face, only a few inches away, the beautiful butterfly is hovering. Its apparition makes him think of many things—perhaps first about the dangerous position of the butterfly, for if it should only touch the water, it is certain to be drowned. But it does not touch the water; and he begins to think how clumsy is the man who moves in water compared with the insect that moves in air, and how ugly a man is by comparison with the exquisite creature which the Greeks likened to the soul or ghost of the man. Thinking about ghosts leads him at once to the memory of a certain very dear ghost about which he forthwith begins to dream.

> What if a certain soul
> Which early slipped its sheath,
> And has for its home the whole
> Of heaven, thus look beneath,
>
> Thus watch one who, in the world,
> Both lives and likes life's way,
> Nor wishes the wings unfurled
> That sleep in the worm, they say?
>
> But sometimes when the weather
> Is blue, and warm waves tempt
> To free oneself of tether,
> And try a life exempt
>
> From worldly noise and dust,
> In the sphere which overbrims
> With passion and thought,—why, just
> Unable to fly, one swims!

This is better understood by paraphrase: "I wonder if the soul of a certain person, who lately died, slipped so gently out of the hard sheath of the perishable body—I wonder if she does not look down from her home in the sky upon me, just as that little butterfly is doing at this moment. And I wonder if she laughs at the clumsiness of this poor swimmer, who finds it so much labour even to move through the water, while she can move through whatever she pleases by the simple act of wishing. And this man, strangely enough, does not want to die, and to become a ghost. He likes to live very much; he does not yet desire those soul-wings which are supposed to be growing within the shell of his body, just as the wings of the butterfly begin to grow in the chrysalis. He does not want to die at all. But sometimes he wants to get away from the struggle and the dust of the city, and to be alone with nature; and then, in order to be perfectly alone, he swims. He would like to fly much better; but he can not. However, swimming is very much like flying, only the element of water is thicker than air."

However, more than the poet's words is suggested here. We are really told that what a fine mind desires is spiritual life, pure intellectual life—free from all the trammels of bodily necessity. Is not the swimmer really a symbol of the superior mind in its present condition? Your best swimmer can not live under the water, neither can he rise into the beautiful blue air. He can only keep his head in the air; his body must remain in the grosser element. Well, a great thinker and poet is ever thus—floating between the universe of spirit and the universe of matter. By his mind he belongs to the region of pure mind,—the ethereal state; but the hard necessity of living keeps him down in the world of sense and grossness and struggle. On the other hand the butterfly, freely moving in a finer element, better represents the state of spirit or soul.

What is the use of being dissatisfied with nature? The best we can do is to enjoy in the imagination those things which it is not possible for us to enjoy in fact.

Emancipate through passion
And thought, with sea for sky,
We substitute, in a fashion,
For heaven—poetry;

Which sea, to all intent,
Gives flesh such noon-disport,
As a finer element
Affords the spirit-sort.

Now you see where the poet's vision of a beautiful butterfly has been leading his imagination. The nearest approach which we can make to the act of flying, in the body, is the act of swimming. The nearest approach that we can make to the heavenly condition, mentally, is in poetry. Poetry, imagination, the pleasure of emotional expression—these represent our nearest approach to paradise. Poetry is the sea in which the soul of man can swim even as butterflies can swim in the air, or happy ghosts swim in the finer element of the infinite ether. The last three stanzas of the poem are very suggestive:—

And meantime, yonder streak
Meets the horizon's verge;
That is the land, to seek
If we tire or dread the surge:

Land the solid and safe—
To welcome again (confess!)
When, high and dry, we chafe
The body, and don the dress.

Does she look, pity, wonder
At one who mimics flight,

Some Poems about Insects

>   Swims—heaven above, sea under,
>   Yet always earth in sight?

"Streak", meaning an indistinct line, here refers to the coast far away, as it appears to the swimmer. It is just such a word as a good Japanese painter ought to appreciate in such a relation. In suggesting that the swimmer is glad to return to shore again and get warm, the poet is telling us that however much we may talk about the happiness of spirits in heaven—however much we may praise heaven in poetry—the truth is that we are very fond of this world, we like comfort, we like company, we like human love and human pleasures. There is a good deal of nonsense in pretending that we think heaven is a better place than the world to which we belong. Perhaps it is a better place, but, as a matter of fact, we do not know anything about it; and we should be frightened if we could go beyond a certain distance from the real world which we do know. As he tells us this, the poet begins again to think about the spirit of the dead woman. Is she happy? Is she looking at him—and pitying him as he swims, taking good care not to go too far away from the land? Or is she laughing at him, because in his secret thoughts he confesses that he likes to live—that he does not want to become a pure ghost at the present time?

Evidently a butterfly was quite enough, not only to make Browning's mind think very seriously, but to make that mind teach us the truth and seriousness which may attach to very small things—incidents, happenings of daily life, in any hour and place. I believe that is the greatest English poem we have on the subject of the butterfly.

The idea that a butterfly might be, not merely the symbol of the soul, but in very fact the spirit of a dead person, is somewhat foreign to English thought; and whatever exists in poetry on the subject must necessarily be quite new. The idea of a relation between insects, birds, or other living creatures, and the spirits of the dead, is enormously old in Oriental literature;—we find it in Sanscrit texts thousands of years ago. But the Western mind has not been accustomed to think of spiritual life as outside of man; and much of natural poetry has consequently remained undeveloped in Western countries. A strange little poem, "The White Moth", is an exception to the general rule that I have indicated; but I am almost certain that its author, A.T. Quiller-Couch, must have read Oriental books, or obtained his fancy from some Eastern source. As the knowledge of Indian literature becomes more general in England, we may expect to find poetry much influenced by Oriental ideas. At the present time, such a composition as this is quite a strange anomaly.

If a leaf rustled, she would start:
And yet she died, a year ago.
How had so frail a thing the heart
To journey where she trembled so?
And do they turn and turn in fright,
Those little feet, in so much night?

The light above the poet's head
Streamed on the page and on the cloth,
And twice and thrice there buffeted
On the black pane a white-winged moth:
'Twas Annie's soul that beat outside,
And "Open, open, open!" cried:

"I could not find the way to God;
There were too many flaming suns
For signposts, and the fearful road

Some Poems about Insects

Led over wastes where millions
Of tangled comets hissed and burned—
I was bewildered and I turned.

"Oh, it was easy then! I knew
Your window and no star beside.
Look up and take me back to you!"
—He rose and thrust the window wide.
'Twas but because his brain was hot
With rhyming; for he heard her not.

But poets polishing a phrase
Show anger over trivial things;
And as she blundered in the blaze
Towards him, on ecstatic wings,
He raised a hand and smote her dead;
Then wrote "*That I had died instead!*"

The lover, or bereaved husband, is writing a poem of which a part is given in the first stanza—which is therefore put in italics. The action proper begins with the second stanza. The soul of the dead woman taps at the window in the shape of a night-butterfly or moth—imagining, perhaps, that she has still a voice and can make herself heard by the man that she loves. She tells the story of her wandering in space—privileged to pass to heaven, yet afraid of the journey. Now the subject of the poem which the lover happens to be writing inside the room is a memory of the dead woman—mourning for her, describing her in exquisite ways. He can not hear her at all; he does not hear even the beating of the little wings at the window, but he stands up and opens the window—because he happens to feel hot and tired. The moth thinks that he has heard her, that he knows; and she flies toward him in great delight. But he, thinking that it is only a troublesome insect, kills her with a blow of his hand; and then sits down to continue his poem with the words, "Oh, how I wish I could have died instead of that dear woman!" Altogether this is a queer poem in English literature, and I believe almost alone of its kind. But it is queer only because of its rarity of subject. As for construction, it is very good indeed.

I do not know that it is necessary to quote any more poems upon butterflies or moths. There are several others; but the workmanship and the thought are not good enough or original enough to justify their use here as class texts. So I shall now turn to the subject of dragon-flies.

Here we must again be very brief. References to dragon-flies are common throughout English poetry, but the references signify little more than a mere colourless mention of the passing of the insect. However, it so happens that the finest modern lines of pure description written about any insect, are about dragon-flies. And they also happen to be by Tennyson. Naturalists and men of science have greatly praised these lines, because of their truth to nature and the accuracy of observation which they show. You will find them in the poem entitled "The Two Voices".

> To-day I saw the dragon-fly
> Come from the wells where he did lie.
>
> An inner impulse rent the veil
> Of his old husk; from head to tail
> Came out clear plates of sapphire mail.
>
> He dried his wings; like gauze they grew;
> Thro' crofts and pastures wet with dew
> A living rush of light he flew.

Some Poems about Insects

There are very few real poems, however, upon the dragon-fly in English, and considering the extraordinary beauty and grace of the insect, this may appear strange to you. But I think that you can explain the strangeness at a later time. The silence of English poets on the subject of insects as compared with Japanese poets is due to general causes that we shall consider at the close of the lecture.

Common flies could scarcely seem to be a subject for poetry—disgusting and annoying creatures as they are. But there are more poems about the house-fly than about the dragon-fly. Last year I quoted for you a remarkable and rather mystical composition by the poet Blake about accidentally killing a fly. Blake represents his own thoughts about the brevity of human life which had been aroused by the incident. It is charming little poem; but it does not describe the fly at all. I shall not quote it here again, because we shall have many other things to talk about; but I shall give you the text of a famous little composition by Oldys on the same topic. It has almost the simplicity of Blake,—and certainly something of the same kind of philosophy.

> Busy, curious, thirsty fly,
> Drink with me and drink as I;
> Freely welcome to my cup,
> Couldst thou sip and sip it up:
> Make the most of life you may,
> Life is short and wears away.
>
> Both alike are mine and thine
> Hastening quick to their decline:
> Thine's a summer, mine's no more,
> Though repeated to threescore.
> Threescore summers, when they're gone,
> Will appear as short as one!

The suggestion is that, after all, time is only a very relative affair in the cosmic order of things. The life of the man of sixty years is not much longer than the life of the insect which lives but a few hours, days, or months. Had Oldys, who belongs to the eighteenth century, lived in our own time, he might have been able to write something very much more curious on this subject. It is now known that time, to the mind of an insect, must appear immensely longer than it appears to the mind of a man. It has been calculated that a mosquito or a gnat moves its wings between four and five hundred times a second. Now the scientific dissection of such an insect, under the microscope, justifies the opinion that the insect must be conscious of each beat of the wings—just as a man feels that he lifts his arm or bends his head every time that the action is performed. A man can not even imagine the consciousness of so short an interval of time as the five-hundredth part of one second. But insect consciousness can be aware of such intervals; and a single day of life might well appear to the gnat as long as the period of a month to a man. Indeed, we have reason to suppose that to even the shortest-lived insect life does not appear short at all; and that the ephemeral may actually, so far as feeling is concerned, live as long as a man—although its birth and death does occur between the rising and the setting of the sun.

We might suppose that bees would form a favourite subject of poetry, especially in countries where agriculture is practised upon such a scale as in England. But such is not really the case. Nearly every English poet makes some reference to bees, as Tennyson does in the famous couplet:—

The moan of doves in immemorial elms,
And murmuring of innumerable bees.

Some Poems about Insects

But the only really remarkable poem addressed to a bee is by the American philosopher Emerson. The poem in question can not be compared as to mere workmanship with some others which I have cited; but as to thinking, it is very interesting, and you must remember that the philosopher who writes poetry should be judged for his thought rather than for the measure of his verse. The whole is not equally good, nor is it short enough to quote entire; I shall only give the best parts.

> Burly, dozing humble-bee,
> Where thou art is clime for me.

* * * * *

> Zigzag steerer, desert cheerer,
> Let me chase thy waving lines;
> Keep me nearer, me thy hearer,
> Singing over shrubs and vines.
>
> Insect lover of the sun,
> Joy of thy dominion!
> Sailor of the atmosphere;
> Swimmer through the waves of air;
> Voyager of light and noon;
> Epicurean of June;
> Wait, I prithee, till I come
> Within earshot of thy hum,—
> All without is martyrdom.

* * * * *

> Thou, in sunny solitudes,
> Rover of the underwoods,

The green silence dost displace
With thy mellow, breezy bass.

* * * * *

Aught unsavoury or unclean
Hath my insect never seen;

* * * * *

Wiser far than human seer,
Yellow-breeched philosopher!
Seeing only what is fair,
Sipping only what is sweet,
Thou dost mock at fate and care,
Leave the chaff, and take the wheat.

This is really the poetry of the bee—visiting only beautiful flowers, and sucking from them their perfumed juices—always healthy, happy, and surrounded by beautiful things. A great rover, a constant wanderer is the bee—visiting many different places, seeing many different things, but stopping only to enjoy what is beautiful to the sight and sweet to the taste. Now Emerson tells us that a wise man should act like the bee—never stopping to look at what is bad, or what is morally ugly, but seeking only what is beautiful and nourishing for the mind. It is a very fine thought; and the manner of expressing it is greatly helped by Emerson's use of curious and forcible words—such as "burly", "zigzag", and the famous expression "yellow-breeched philosopher"—which has passed almost into an American household phrase. The allusion of course is to the thighs of the bee, covered with the yellow pollen of flowers so as to make them seem covered with yellow breeches, or trousers reaching only to the knees.

I do not of course include in the lecture such child songs about insects as that famous one beginning with the words, "How doth the little busy bee improve each shining hour." This is no doubt didactically very good; but I wish to offer you only examples of really fine poetry on the topic. Therefore leaving the subject of bees for the time, let us turn to the subject of musical insects—the singers of the fields and woods—grasshoppers and crickets.

In Japanese poetry there are thousands of verses upon such insects. Therefore it seems very strange that we have scarcely anything on the subject in English. And the little that we do have is best represented by the poem of Keats on the night cricket. The reference is probably to what we call in England the hearth cricket, an insect which hides in houses, making itself at home in some chink of the brickwork or stonework about a fireplace, for it loves the warmth. I suppose that the small number of poems in English about crickets can be partly explained by the scarcity of night singers. Only the house cricket seems to be very well known. But on the other hand, we can not so well explain the rarity of composition in regard to the daysingers—the grasshoppers and locusts which can be heard, though somewhat faintly, in any English country place after sunset during the warm season. Another queer thing is that the example set by Keats has not been imitated or at least followed even up to the present time.

> The poetry of earth is never dead:
> When all the birds are faint with the hot sun, etc.

In this charming composition you will have noticed the word "stove"; but you must remember that this is not a stove as we understand the term now, and signifies only an old-fashioned fireplace of brick or tile. In Keats's day there were no iron stoves. Another word which I want to notice is the word "poetry" in the first line. By the poetry of nature the poet means the voices of nature—the musical sounds made by its idle life in woods and fields. So the word "poetry" here has especially the meaning of song, and corresponds very closely to the Japanese word which signifies either poem or song, but perhaps more especially the latter. The general meaning of the sonnet is that at no time, either in winter or in summer, is nature silent. When the birds do not sing, the grasshoppers make music for us; and when the cold has killed or banished all other life, then the house cricket begins with its thin sweet song to make us think of the dead voices of the summer.

There is not much else of note about the grasshopper and the cricket in the works of the great English poets. But perhaps you do not know that Tennyson in his youth took up the subject and made a long poem upon the grasshopper, but suppressed it after the edition of 1842. He did not think it good enough to rank with his other work. But a few months ago the poems which Tennyson suppressed in the final edition of his works have been published and carefully edited by an eminent scholar, and among these poems we find "The Grasshopper". I will quote some of this poem, because it is beautiful, and because the fact of its suppression will serve to show you how very exact and careful Tennyson was to preserve only the very best things that he wrote.

> Voice of the summer wind,
> Joy of the summer plain,
> Life of the summer hours,
> Carol clearly, bound along,

No Tithon thou as poets feign
(Shame fall 'em, they are deaf and blind),
But an insect lithe and strong
Bowing the seeded summer flowers.
Prove their falsehood and thy quarrel,
Vaulting on thine airy feet
Clap thy shielded sides and carol,
Carol clearly, chirrups sweet.
Thou art a mailed warrior in youth and strength complete;
    Armed cap-a-pie,
    Full fair to see;
    Unknowing fear,
    Undreading loss,
    A gallant cavalier,
Sans peur et sans reproche.
    In sunlight and in shadow,
    The Bayard of the meadow.

The reference to Tithonus is a reference of course to a subject afterwards beautifully elaborated in another poem by Tennyson, the great poem of "Tithonus". The Bayard here referred to was the great French model of perfect chivalry, and is sometimes called the last of the feudal knights. He was said to be without fear and without blame. You may remember that he was killed by a ball from a gun —it was soon after the use of artillery in war had been introduced; and his dying words were to the effect that he feared there was now an end of great deeds, because men had begun to fight from a distance with machines instead of fighting in the old knightly and noble way with sword and spear. The grasshopper, covered with green plates and bearing so many little sharp spines upon its long limbs, seems to have suggested to Tennyson the idea of a fairy knight in green armour.

Insect Literature

As I said before, England is poor in singing insects, while America is rich in them—almost, perhaps, as rich as Japan, although you will not find as many different kinds of singing insects in any one state or district. The singing insects of America are peculiar to particular localities. But the Eastern states have perhaps the most curious insect of this kind. It is called the Katydid. This name is spelt either Katydid, or Catydid—though the former spelling is preferable. Katy, or Katie, is the abbreviation of the name Catherine; very few girls are called by the full name Catherine, also spelt Katherine; because the name is long and unmusical, their friends address them usually as Katy, and their acquaintances, as Kate. Well, the insect of which I am speaking, a kind of *sémi*, makes a sound resembling the sound of the words "Katie did!" Hence the name—one of the few corresponding to the names given to the Japanese *sémi*, such as *tsuku-tsuku-boshi*, or *minmin-sémi*. The most interesting composition upon this cicada is by Oliver Wendell Holmes, but it is of the lighter sort of verse, with a touch of humour in it. I shall quote a few verses only, as the piece contains some allusions that would require explanation at considerable length.

> I love to hear thine earnest voice,
>   Wherever thou art hid,
> Thou testy little dogmatist,
>   Thou pretty Katydid!
> Thou mindest me of gentlefolks,—
>   Old gentlefolks are they,—
> Thou say'st an undisputed thing
>   In such a solemn way.

*   *   *   *   *

Some Poems about Insects

Oh tell me where did Katy live,
    And what did Katy do?
And was she very fair and young,
    And yet so wicked, too?
Did Katy love a naughty man,
    Or kiss more cheeks than one?
I warrant Katy did no more
    Than many a Kate has done.

*   *   *   *   *

Ah, no! The living oak shall crash,
    That stood for ages still,
The rock shall rend its mossy base
    And thunder down the hill,
Before the little Katydid
    Shall add one word, to tell
The mystic story of the maid
    Whose name she knows so well.

The word "testy" may be a little unfamiliar to some of you; it is a good old-fashioned English term for "cross", "irritable". The reference to the "old gentlefolks" implies the well-known fact that in argument old persons are inclined to be much more obstinate than young people. And there is also a hint in the poem of the tendency among old ladies to blame the conduct of young girls even more severely than may be necessary. There is nothing else to recommend the poem except its wit and the curiousness of the subject. There are several other verses about the same creature, by different American poets; but none of them is quite so good as the composition of Holmes. However, I may cite a few verses from one of the earlier American poets, Philip Freneau, who flourished in the eighteenth century and the early part of the nineteenth. He long anticipated the fancy of Holmes; but he spells the word Catydid.

> In a branch of willow hid
> Sings the evening Catydid:
> From the lofty locust bough
> Feeding on a drop of dew,
> In her suit of green arrayed
> Hear her singing in the shade—
> 　　Catydid, Catydid, Catydid!
>
> While upon a leaf you tread,
> Or repose your little head
> On your sheet of shadows laid,
> All the day you nothing said;
> Half the night your cheery tongue
> Revelled out its little song,—
> 　　Nothing else but Catydid.
>
> * 　 * 　 * 　 * 　 *
>
> Tell me, what did Caty do?
> Did she mean to trouble you?
> Why was Caty not forbid
> To trouble little Catydid?
> Wrong, indeed, at you to fling,
> Hurting no one while you sing,—
> 　　Catydid! Catydid! Catydid!

To Dr. Holmes the voice of the cicada seemed like the voice of an old obstinate woman, an old prude, accusing a young girl of some fault,—but to Freneau the cry of the little creature seemed rather to be like the cry of a little child complaining—a little girl, perhaps, complaining that somebody had been throwing stones at her, or had hurt her in some way. And, of course, the unfinished character of the phrase allows equally well either supposition.

Before going back to more serious poetry, I want—while we are speaking of American poets—to make one reference to the ironical or satirical poetry which insects have inspired in some minds, taking for example the poem by Charlotte Perkins Stetson about a butterfly. This author is rather a person of note, being a prominent figure in educational reforms and the author of a volume of poems of a remarkably strong kind in the didactic sense. In other words, she is especially a moral poet; and unless moral poetry be really very well executed, it is scarcely worth while classing it as literature. I think, however, that the symbolism in the following verses will interest you—especially when we comment upon them. The composition from which they are taken is entitled "A Conservative".

The poet, walking in the garden one morning, sees a butterfly, very unhappy, and gifted with power to express the reason of its unhappiness. The butterfly says, complaining of its wings,

> "My legs are thin and few
> Where once I had a swarm!
> Soft fuzzy fur—a joy to view—
> Once kept my body warm,
> Before these flapping wing-things grew,
> To hamper and deform!"
>
> At that outrageous bug I shot
> The fury of mine eye;
> Said I, in scorn all burning hot,
> In rage and anger high,

"You ignominious idiot!
Those wings are made to fly!"

"I do not want to fly," said he,
"I only want to squirm!"
And he drooped his wings dejectedly,
But still his voice was firm:
"I do not want to be a fly!
I want to be a worm!"

O yesterday of unknown lack!
To-day of unknown bliss!
I left my fool in red and black,
The last I saw was this,—
The creature madly climbing back
Into his chrysalis.

Of course the wings here represent the powers of the mind—knowledge, reason, will. Men ought to use these in order to reach still nobler and higher states of life. But there are men who refuse to use their best faculties for this end. Such men are like butterflies who do not want to take the trouble to fly, but prefer the former condition of the caterpillar which does nothing but eat and sleep. As applied to certain forms of conservatism the satire is strong.

Something may now be said as to poems about spiders. But let me remind you that a spider is not an insect. Scientifically it has no relation to the great family of true insects; it belongs to the very distinct family of the arthropoda or "joint-footed" animals. But as it is still popularly called an insect in most European countries, we may be excused for including it in the subject of the present lecture. I suppose you know that one of the scientific names for this whole class of creatures is Arachnida,—a name derived from the Greek name Arachne. The story of Arachne is interesting, and everybody studying natural history ought to know it. Arachne was a young girl, according to the Greek story, who was very skilful at weaving. She wove cloths of many different colours and beautiful patterns, and everybody admired her work. This made her vain—so vain that at last she said that even the goddess of weaving could not weave better than she. Immediately after she had said that, the terrible goddess herself—Pallas Athena—entered the room. Pallas Athena was not only the goddess of wisdom, you know, but especially the goddess of young girls, presiding over the chastity, the filial piety, and the domestic occupations of virgins; and she was very angry at the conceit of this girl. So she said to her, "You have boasted that you can weave as well as I can; now let me see you weave!" So Arachne was obliged to sit down at her loom and weave in the presence of the goddess; and the goddess also wove, far surpassing the weaving of Arachne. When the weaving was done, the goddess asked the girl, "Now see! which is the better, my work or yours?" And Arachne was obliged to confess that she had been defeated and put to shame. But the goddess was not thoroughly satisfied; to punish Arachne, she touched her lightly with the distaff, saying, "Spin forever!" and thereupon Arachne was changed into a spider, which forever spins and weaves perishable films of perishable shiny thread. Poetically we still may call a spider Arachne.

I have here a little poem of a touching character entitled "Arachne", by Rose Terry Cooke,—one of the symbolic poems which are becoming so numerous in these days of newer and deeper philosophy. I think that you will like it: a spinster, that is, a maiden passed the age of girlhood, is the speaker.

I watch her in the corner there,
As, restless, bold, and unafraid,
She slips and floats along the air
Till all her subtle house is made.

Her home, her bed, her daily food,
All from that hidden store she draws;
She fashions it and knows it good,
By instinct's strong and sacred laws.

No tenuous threads to weave her nest,
She seeks and gathers there or here;
But spins it from her faithful breast,
Renewing still, till leaves are sere.

Then, worn with toil, and tired of life,
In vain her shining traps are set.
Her frost hath hushed the insect strife
And gilded flies her charm forget.

But swinging in the snares she spun,
She sways to every wintry wind:
Her joy, her toil, her errand done,
Her corse the sport of storms unkind.

The symbolism of these verses will appear to you more significant when I tell you that it refers especially to conditions in New England in the present period. The finest American population—perhaps the finest Anglo-Saxons ever produced—were the New Englanders of the early part of the century. But with the growth of the new century, the men found themselves attracted elsewhere, especially westward; their shrewdness, their energies, their inventiveness, were needed in newer regions. And they wandered away by thousands and thousands, never to come back again, and leaving the women behind them. Gradually the place of these men was taken by immigrants of inferior development—but the New England women had nothing to hope for from these strangers. The bravest of them also went away to other states; but myriads who could not go were condemned by circumstances to stay and earn their living by hard work without any prospect of happy marriage. The difficulty which a girl of culture may experience in trying to live by the work of her hands in New England is something not easily imagined. But it is getting to be the same in most Western countries. Such a girl is watching a spider weaving in the corner of the same room where she herself is weaving; and she thinks, "Am I not like that spider, obliged to supply my every need by the work of my own hands, without sympathy, without friends? The spider will spin and catch flies until the autumn comes; then she will die. Perhaps I too must continue to spin until the autumn of my own life—until I become too old to work hard, and die of cold and of exhaustion."

> Poor sister of the spinster clan!
> I too from out my store within
> My daily life and living plan,
> My home, my rest, my pleasure spin.
>
> I know thy heart when heartless hands
> Sweep all that hard-earned web away;
> Destroy its pearled and glittering bands,
> And leave thee homeless by the way.
>
> I know thy peace when all is done.
> Each anchored thread, each tiny knot,

Soft shining in the autumn sun;
A sheltered, silent, tranquil lot.

I know what thou hast never known,—
Sad presage to a soul allowed—
That not for life I spin, alone,
But day by day I spin my shroud.

The reference to the sweeping away of the spider's web, of course, implies the pain often caused to such hardworking girls by the meanness of men who employ them only to cheat them—shopkeepers or manufacturers who take their work without justly paying for it, and who criticise it as bad in order to force the owner to accept less money than it is worth. Again a reference may be intended to the destruction of the home by some legal trick—some unscrupulous method of cheating the daughter out of the property bequeathed to her by her parents.

Notice a few pretty words here. The "pearled" as applied to the spider's thread gives an intimation of the effect produced by dew on the thread, but there is also the suggestion of tears upon the thread work woven by the hands of the girl. The participle "anchored" is very pretty in its use here as an adjective, because this word is now especially used for rope-fastening, whether the rope be steel or hemp; and particularly for the fastening of the cables of a bridge. The last stanza might be paraphrased thus: "Sister Spider, I know more than you—and that knowledge makes me unhappy. You do not know, when you are spinning your little web, that you are really weaving your own shroud. But I know this, my work is slowly but surely killing me. And I know it because I have a soul—at least a mind made otherwise than yours."

The use of the word "soul" in the last stanza of this poem,

Some Poems about Insects

brings me back to the question put forth in an earlier part of the lecture—why European poets, during the last two thousand years, have written so little upon the subject of insects? Three thousand, four thousand years ago, the most beautiful Greek poetry—poetry more perfect than anything of English poetry—was written upon insects. In old Japanese literature poems upon insects are to be found by thousands. What is the signification of the great modern silence in Western countries upon this delightful topic? I believe that Christianity, as dogma, accounts for the long silence. The opinions of the early Church refused soul, ghost, intelligence of any sort to other creatures than man. All animals were considered as automata—that is, as self-acting machines, moved by a something called instinct, for want of a better name. To talk about the souls of animals or the spirits of animals would have been very dangerous in the Middle Ages, when the Church had supreme power; it would indeed have been to risk or to invite an accusation of witchcraft, for demons were then thought to take the shape of animals at certain times. To discuss the *mind* of an animal would have been for the Christian faith to throw doubt upon the existence of human souls as taught by the Church; for if you grant that animals are able to think, then you must acknowledge that man is able to think without a soul, or you must acknowledge that the soul is not the essential principle of thought and action. Until after the time of Descartes, who later argued philosophically that animals were only machines, it was scarcely possible to argue rationally about the matter in Europe.

Nevertheless, we shall soon perceive that this explanation will not cover all the facts. You will naturally ask how it happens that, if the question be a question of animal souls, birds, horses, dogs, cats, and many other animals have been made the subject of Western poems from ancient times. The silence is only upon the subject of insects. And, again, Christianity has one saint—the most beautiful character in all Christian hagiography—who thought of all nature in a manner that, at first sight, strangely resembles Buddhism. This saint was Francis of Assisi, born in the latter part of the twelfth century, so that he may be said to belong to the very heart of the Middle Ages,—the most superstitious epoch of Christianity. Now this saint used to talk to trees and stones as if they were animated beings. He addressed the sun as "my brother sun"; and he spoke of the moon as his sister. He preached not only to human beings, but also to the birds and the fishes; and he made a great many poems on these subjects, full of a strange and childish beauty. For example, his sermon to the doves, beginning, "My little sisters, the doves," in which he reminds them that their form is the emblem or symbol of the Holy Ghost, is a beautiful poem; and has been, with many others, translated into nearly all modern languages. But observe that neither St. Francis nor any other saint has anything to say on the subject of insects.

Perhaps we must go back further than Christianity to guess the meaning of these distinctions. Among the ancient races of Asia, where the Jewish faith arose, there were strange and sinister beliefs about insects—old Assyrian superstitions, old Babylonian beliefs. Insects seemed to those early peoples very mysterious creatures (which they really are); and it appears to have been thought that they had a close relation to the world of demons and evil spirits. I suppose you know that the name of one of their gods, Beelzebub, signifies the Lord of Flies. The Jews, as is shown by their Talmudic literature, inherited some of these ideas; and it is quite probable that they were passed

Some Poems about Insects

on to the days of Christianity. Again, in the early times of Christianity in Northern Africa the Church had to fight against superstitions of an equally strange sort derived from old Egyptian beliefs. Among the Egyptians, certain insects were sacred and became symbols of divinity,—such as the beetle. Now I imagine that for these reasons the subject of insects became at an early time a subject which Christianity thought dangerous, and that thereafter a kind of hostile opinion prevailed regarding any literature upon this topic.

However, to-day things are very different. With the development of scientific studies—especially of microscopic study—it has been found that insects, far from being the lowliest of creatures, are the most highly organised of all beings; that their special senses are incomparably superior to our own; and that in natural history, from the evolutional standpoint, they have to be given first place. This of course renders it impossible any longer to consider the insect as a trifling subject. Moreover, the new philosophy is teaching the thinking classes in all Western countries the great truth of the unity of life. With the recognition of such unity, an insect must interest the philosophers—even the man of ordinary culture—quite as much as the bird or any other animal.

Nearly all the poems which I have quoted to you have been poems of very modern date—from which we may infer that interest in the subject of insects has been developing of late years only. In this connection it is interesting to note that a very religious poet, Whittier, gave us in the last days of his life a poem upon ants. This would have seemed strange enough in a former age; it does not seem strange to-day, and it is beautiful. The subject is taken from old Jewish literature.

"King Solomon and the Ants"

Out from Jerusalem
    The King rode with his great
      War chiefs and lords of state,
And Sheba's queen with them;

Comely, but black withal,
    To whom, perchance, belongs
      That wondrous Song of Songs,
Sensuous and mystical,

Whereto devout souls turn
    In fond, ecstatic dream,
      And through its earth-born theme
The Love of Loves discern.

Proud in the Syrian sun,
    In gold and purple sheen,
      The dusky Ethiop queen
Smiled on King Solomon.

Wisest of men, he knew
    The languages of all
      The creatures great or small
That trod the earth or flew.

Across an ant-hill led
    The king's path, and he heard
      Its small folk, and their word
He thus interpreted:

"Here comes the king men greet
    As wise and good and just,

> To crush us in the dust
> Under his heedless feet."

The king, understanding the language of insects, turns to the queen and explains to her what the ants have just said. She advises him to pay no attention to the sarcasm of the ants—how dare such vile creatures speak thus about a king! But Solomon thinks otherwise:

> "Nay," Solomon replied,
>   "The wise and strong should seek
>   The welfare of the weak,"
> And turned his horse aside.
>
> His train, with quick alarm,
>   Curved with their leader round
>   The ant-hill's peopled mound,
> And left it free from harm.
>
> The jewelled head bent low;
>   "Oh, king!" she said, "henceforth
>   The secret of thy worth
> And wisdom well I know.
>
> "Happy must be the State
>   Whose ruler heedeth more
>   The murmurs of the poor
> Than flatteries of the great."

The reference to the Song of Songs—also the Song of Solomon and Canticle of Canticles—may require a little explanation. The line "Comely but black withal", is borrowed from a verse of this song—"I am black but beautiful, oh, ye daughters of Jerusalem, as the tents of Kedar, as the curtains of Solomon." In another part of the song the reason of this blackness is given: "I am black, because the sun hath looked upon me." From which we can see that the word black only means dark, brown, tanned by the sun. Perhaps you do not know that as late as the middle of the eighteenth century it was still the custom in England to speak of a person with black hair and eyes as "a black man"—a custom which Charles Lamb had reason to complain of even at a later day. The tents referred to in the text were probably tents made of camel-skin, such as the Arabs still make, and the colour of these is not black but brown. Whether Solomon wrote the so-called song or not we do not know; but the poet refers to a legend that it was written in praise of the beauty of the dark queen who came from Sheba to visit the wisest man of the world. Such is not, however, the opinion of modern scholars. The composition is really dramatic, although thrown into lyrical form, and as arranged by Renan and others it becomes a beautiful little play, of which each act is a monologue. "Sensuous" the poet correctly calls it; for it is a form of praise of woman's beauty in all its details, as appears in such famous verses as these: "How beautiful are thy feet in shoes, O prince's daughter; the joints of thy thighs are like jewels, the work of the hands of a cunning workman. Thy two breasts are like two young roes that are twins which feed among the lilies." But Christianity, instead of dismissing this part of the Bible, interpreted the song mystically—insisting that the woman described meant the Church, and the lover, Christ. Of course only very pious people continue to believe this; even the good Whittier preferred the legend that it was written about the Queen of Sheba.

I suppose that I ought to end this lecture upon insect poetry by some quotation to which a moral or philosophical meaning can be attached. I shall end it therefore with a quotation from the poet Gray. The poetry of insects may be said to have first appeared in English literature during the second half of the eighteenth century, so that it is only, at the most, one hundred and fifty years old. But the first really fine poem of the eighteenth century relating to the subject is quite as good as anything since composed by Englishmen upon insect life in general. Perhaps Gray referred especially to what we call May-flies—those delicate ghostly insects which hover above water surfaces in fine weather, but which die on the same day that they are born. He does not specify May-flies, however, and we may consider the moral of the poem quite apart from any particular kind of insect. You will find this reference in the piece entitled "Ode on the Spring", in the third, fourth, and fifth stanzas.

> Still is the toiling hand of care:
>   The panting herds repose:
> Yet hark, how through the peopled air
>   The busy murmur glows!
> The insect youth are on the wing,
> Eager to taste the honied spring,
> And float amid the liquid noon:
> Some lightly o'er the current skim,
> Some show their gaily-gilded trim
>   Quick-glancing to the sun.
>
> To Contemplation's sober eye
>   Such is the race of man:
> And they that creep, and they that fly,
>   Shall end where they began.
> Alike the Busy and the Gay
> But flutter through life's little day,

In fortune's varying colours dressed:
Brushed by the hand of rough Mischance,
Or chilled by Age, their airy dance
    They leave, in dust to rest.

Methinks I hear in accents low
    The sportive kind reply:
Poor moralist! and what art thou?
    A solitary fly!
Thy joys no glittering female meets,
No hive hast thou of hoarded sweets,
No painted plumage to display:
On hasty wings thy youth is flown;
Thy sun is set; thy spring is gone—
    We frolic, while 'tis May.

The poet Gray was never married, and the last stanza which I have quoted refers jocosely to himself. It is an artistic device to set off the moral by a little mockery, so that it may not appear too melancholy. Seeing the insects sporting in the bright weather, but all doomed so soon to die, the poet first thinks:

"Well, men are just insects after all, in the eternal order of things. Some insects can only creep, while others can fly; some insects can store up honey or grain; some live only a few hours: some live for a season. In like manner, some men are stupid and are unable to succeed in the world; whereas others rise to honour, accumulate wealth, reach honoured old age and see their children prosper. But the end is the same for all men, as it is for the insect,—dust." But then the poet fancies that he hears the voice of the insects reproaching him, and asking him: "What are you yourself, compared with an insect? You are not, perhaps, quite so good as an insect. For the insect at least fulfils its life upon earth; the male finds its female; the honey or the grain is stored up; and the joy of life is found by us. But you—what have you done in this world? You have no wife; you have no treasures; you have had no real part in the enjoyment of this world. And therefore however you may moralise, perhaps you are not worthy to compare yourself even with the bee or the ant or the dragon-fly that does its little duty in this impermanent state of existence."

蟲とギリシアの詩
Insects and Greek Poetry

The subject which I have chosen for to-day's lecture might seem to you rather remote from the topic of English literature, at least, from the topic of English literature as taught in Japan. Here the Chinese language represents, in your long course of studies, what Greek and Latin represent to the English student. But in England, or in any advanced European country, the subject would not be remote from the study of the native literature, because that is carried on from first to last upon a classical foundation. Any good Greek scholar knows something about the Greek poetry on the subject of insects, and knows how to use that poetry in compositions of his own; so I think that this departure from our routine work is quite justified, and I believe that you will find the subject interesting.

Last year, when lecturing about Keats's poems, I remarked to you that he was one of the very few English poets who wrote about singing insects—I refer, of course, to his poem on the cricket. Most modern European poetry is barren on the subject of crickets, cicadae, and insects generally—with the exception of butterflies and bees. Tennyson, indeed, has given attention to dragon-flies and other insects. But, as a rule, it is not to European poetry of modern times that we can look for anything of an interesting kind in regard to musical insects. We must go back

Insects and Greek Poetry

to the old Greek civilisation for that. You know that the old Greeks were endowed far beyond any modern races of the West: their literature, their arts, their conception of life, have never been equalled in later times, and probably will not be equalled again for thousands of years. And it should be interesting to the Japanese student of literature to know that his own people accord with the old Greeks in their appreciation of insect music as one of the great charms of country life.

Most of the Greek poems about insects are to be found in what is called the Greek Anthology. Besides the distinct works of great authors which have come down to us, there have been preserved collections of very short poems—collections which were made by the Greek, themselves, or by Greek scholars of a later day, many centuries ago. None of these collections are complete: a great deal has been lost—to the eternal regret of all lovers of poetry. But those that we have represent an immense variety of little poems upon an immense variety of subjects; and among these are a number of poems about insects. To-day I want to quote some of these to you, in an English prose translation. There are many poetical translations, also; but no modern poet can reproduce the real charm of the Greek verse. Therefore it is just as well that we should read only the plain prose.

The greater number of these poems are between two thousand and twenty-five hundred years old. Some of them were composed in cities that no longer exist; some of them were written by persons whose names have been lost forever; this makes them all the more precious. They show us how very much like modern human nature was the human nature of those vanished people. And they show us also that there were many points of resemblance in the old Greek and in the Japanese character.

Insect Literature

It is possible that the Greeks used to keep insects in cages, for the pleasure of hearing them sing. We have in the first Idyll of Theocritus a description of a boy taking charge of a vineyard to protect the grapes from the foxes, and occupying his time by "plaiting a pretty locust-cage with stalks of asphodel, and fitting it with reeds". Also we have in one of the poems of Meleager a reference to the feeding of crickets with leeks cut up very small—which would seem to show that the experience of Greeks and Japanese in the feeding of certain kinds of insects was much the same. A leek, you know, is a kind of small onion, and the soft inner part of a similar plant is used in Tōkyō to-day by insect-feeders.

The poems refer principally to cicadae, musical grasshoppers, and some kinds of night crickets, and these three classes of musical insects correspond tolerably well to three classes of Japanese musical insects. But whereas, in Japan, the sound made by the sémi is considered to be too loud in most cases to be musical, it is especially the cicada that is celebrated in the Greek poem. This fact would not, however, indicate a real difference in the musical taste of the two races; it would rather indicate a difference in the species of the insect. Probably the Greek sémi were much less noisy than their relations in the Far East. But, at the same time, perhaps most beautiful of all the Greek poems about insects is a poem about a night cricket. It is attributed to Meleager—one of the sweetest singers of the later Greek literature.

"O thou cricket that cheatest me of my regrets, the soother of slumber;—O thou cricket that art the muse of ploughed fields, and art with shrill wings the self-formed imitation of the lyre, chirrup me something pleasant, while beating thy vocal wings with thy feet. How I wish, O cricket, that thou wouldst release me from the troubles of much sleepless care, weaving the thread of a voice that causes love to wander away! And I will give thee for morning gifts a leek ever fresh, and drops of dew, cut up small for thy mouth."

The great beauty of this little piece is in the line about "weaving the thread of a voice that causes love to wander away"; listening to the charm of the insect's song at night, the poet is able to forget his troubles. The expression, "thread of a voice", exquisitely represents what we would call to-day the *thin* quality of the little creature's song. It is also evident that the Greeks observed such insects very closely and noticed how their music was made. The cricket is correctly described as striking its wings with its feet. But in the cicada the stridulatory organ is not in the wings but in the breast; and the old poets observed this fact also.

It would also appear that Greek children kept insects as pets, and made little graves for them when they died, just as one sees Japanese children doing to-day. Here is a little poem twenty-six hundred years old, written by a Greek girl of Sicily, a poetess named Anyte. It is the epitaph of a locust and a tettix—by which word we may understand cicada. "For a locust, the nightingale amongst ploughed fields, and for the tettix, whose bed is in the oak, did Myro make a common tomb, after the damsel had dropped a maiden tear; for Hades, hard to be persuaded, had gone away, taking with her two playthings."

How freshly do the tears of this little girl still shine today, after the passing of twenty-six hundred years! There is another poem on the very same subject, by a later poet, in the Anthology,—also celebrating the grief of Myro.

"For a locust and a tettix has Myro placed this monument, after throwing upon both a little dust with her hands, and weeping affectionately at the funeral pyre; for Hades had carried of the male songster, and Proserpine the other."

But if little girls in old Greece were so tender-hearted as this, I am sorry to tell you that little boys were not. They caught cicadae much as little boys in Tōkyō to-day catch sémi, and they were not very merciful, if we can judge from the following poem, intended to represent the death-song of a cicada:

"No longer shall I delight myself by singing out the song from my quick-moving wings; for I have fallen into the savage hand of a boy, who seized me unexpectedly, as I was sitting under the green leaves."

You must know that the cicada received religious respect in some parts of Greece; it was believed to be the favourite insect of the goddess of Wisdom, and it was often represented in statues of the goddess. I do not mean that the Greeks worshiped it, but they had many religious traditions concerning it. At one time the Athenian women used to wear cicadae of gold in their hair; and this ornament was afterwards adopted by Roman ladies. As for the merits of the insect we have a very curious little poem in which it is celebrated as a favourite of the gods: "We deem thee happy, O cicada, because, having drunk like a king a little dew, thou dost chirrup on the tops of trees. For all those things are thine that thou seest in the fields, and whatever the seasons produce. Yet thou art a friend of land-tillers, to no one doing any harm. Thou art held in honour by mortals as the pleasant harbinger of song. The muses love thee. Phoebus himself loves thee and has gifted thee with a shrill song, and old age does not wear thee down. O thou clever one,—earth-born, song-loving, without suffering, having flesh without blood,—thou art nearly equal to the gods."

Another poet speaks more definitely about the relation of the insect to the goddess of Wisdom—putting his words into the mouth of the insect. "Not only sitting upon lofty trees do I know how to sing, warmed with the great heat of summer, an unpaid minstrel to wayfaring man, and sipping the vapour of dew, that is like woman's milk. But even upon the spear of Athene, with her beautiful helmet, will you see me, the tettix, seated. For as much as we are loved by the Muses, so much is Athene by us. For the virgin has established a prize for melody."

Meleager also celebrates the tettix:

"Thou vocal tettix, drunk with drops of dew, thou singest the muse that lives in the country, thou dost prattle in the desert, and sitting with thy serrated limbs on the tops of petals, thou givest out the melody of the lyre with thy dusky skin! Come thou, O friend, and speak some new playful thing to the wood nymphs, and chirrup a strain responsive to Pan, in order that, after flying from love, I may find mid-day sleep here, reclining under a shady plane tree."

But the most remarkable poem about a cicada in the whole Greek collection is a little piece twenty-three hundred years old, attributed to the poet Evenus. It was written upon the occasion of seeing a nightingale catching a cicada. Evenus calls the nightingale, "Attic maiden", because in Greek mythology the nightingale was a daughter of an ancient king of Attica; her name was Philomela, and she was turned into a bird by the gods out of pity for her great sorrow.

This is the poem:—

"Thou, Attic maiden, honey-fed, hast chirping seized a chirping cicada, and bearest it to thy unfledged young— thou, a twitterer, the twitterer; thou, the winged, the well-winged; thou, a stranger, the stranger; thou, a summer child, the summer child! Wilt thou not quickly throw it away? For it is not right, it is not just, that those engaged in song should perish by the mouths of those engaged in song!"

This poem has been put into English verse by several hands. Most of the verse translations are very disappointing; but in this case one translation happens to be tolerably good, so that we may quote it:—

Honey-nurtured Attic maiden,
Wherefore to thy brood dost wing
With the shrill cicada laden?
'T is, like thee, a prattling thing,
'T is a sojourner and stranger.
And a summer child, like thee.
'T is, like thee, a winged ranger
Of the air's immensity.
From thy bill this instant fling her,—
'T is not proper, just, or good.
That a little ballad-singer
Should be killed for singer's food.

Another ancient poem represents the insect caught in a spider's web and crying there until the poet himself came to the rescue.

"A spider, having woven its thin web with its slim feet, caught a tettix hampered in the intricate net. I did not, however, on seeing the young thing that loves music, run by it, while [it was] making a lament in the thin fetters, but, freeing it from the net, I relieved it, and spoke to it thus, 'Be free, thou who singest with a musical voice!' "

Like the poets of the Far East, the Greek singers especially celebrated the harmlessness of the cicada. We have already had one example in the poem beginning, "We deem you happy", etc., by the great poet Anacreon. Here is another very old composition, of which the authorship is not known.

Insects and Greek Poetry

"Why, O Shepherds, do ye drag, by a shameless captivity, from dewy boughs, me a cicada, the lover of solitude, the roadside songster of the nymphs, chirping shrilly in mid-day heat on the mountains and in the shady groves. Behold the thrush and the blackbird—behold how many starlings are plunderers of the fields! It is right to take the destroyers of fruits. Kill them. What grudging is there of leaves and grassy dew?"

Occasionally, too, we find the Greek poet, like the Japanese, compassionating the insects of autumn, and lamenting for their death. The following example is said to have been composed by an ancient writer called Mnasolcas:

"No more with wings shrill sounding shalt thou sing, O locust, along the fertile furrows settling; nor me reclining under shady foliage shalt thou delight, striking, with dusky wings, a pleasant melody!"

By the word locust here is probably meant a kind of musical grasshopper—of the same class as those insects which are so common in this country. In England and in America the word locust commonly refers to an insect frequenting trees rather than grass.

We may now attempt a few remarks upon the social signification of this old Greek poetry, and its charming suggestion of refined sensibility and kindness.

You will not find Roman poets writing about insects—at least not until a very late day, and then only in imitation of the Greeks. This little fact, insignificant as it may seem, serves us as an illustration of the vast difference in the character of the two races.

Grand in many respects the Romans were—splendid soldiers, matchless architects, excellent rulers. They had all the qualities of power and foresight, and executive ability. But at no time did they ever reach the standard of old Greek refinement,—not even after they had been studying Greek literature and philosophy for hundreds of years. Something of the savage and the ferocious always remained in Roman character, which finally developed into the most monstrous forms of cruelty that the world has ever known, the cruelty of an age when the greatest pleasure of life was the spectacle of death.

On the other hand, even in the times of their degradation under Roman rule, the Greeks could not be coldly cruel. They resisted the introduction of the Roman games into their civilisation; they opposed, whenever it was possible, the sentiment of humanity and pity to gladiatorial shows. A people who enjoyed seeing men killing each other for sport could not have written poems about insects. And a people that wrote poems about insects could not find pleasure in cruelty.

Indeed, I think that the capacity to enjoy the music of insects and all that it signifies in the great poem of nature tells very plainly of goodness of heart, aesthetic sensibility, a perfectly healthy state of mind. All this the Greeks certainly had. What most impresses us in the tone of their literature, in the feeling of their art, in the charm of their conception of life, is the great joyousness of the Greek nature,—a joyousness fresh as that of a child,—combined with a power of deep thinking, in which it had no rival. Those old Greeks, though happy as children and as kindly, were very great philosophers, to whom we go for instruction even at this day. What the world now most feels in need of is the return of that old Greek spirit of happiness and of kindness. We can think deeply enough; but all our thinking only serves, it would seem, to darken our lives instead of brightening them.

Now, as I have said before, there was very much in the old Greek life that resembled the old Japanese life; and there was certainly in old Japan a certain joyousness and gentleness for which the Western World can show no parallel in modern times. We should have to go back to the Greek times for that. Were some great classic scholar, perfectly familiar with the manners and customs of this country, to make a literary study of the parallel between Greek and Japanese life and thought, I am sure that the result would be as surprising as it would be charming. Although the two religions present great differences, the religious spirit offers a great many extraordinary resemblances. It was not only in writing about insects that the Greek poets came close to the Japanese poets: they came close to them also in thousands of little touches of an emotional kind, referring to the gods, the fate of man, the pleasure of festival days, those sorrows of existence also which have been the same in all ages of humanity. I wonder if you remember a little poem in the *Man yo shu*, attributed to a Japanese poet named Okura, in which, lamenting the death of his little son, he begs that the porter of the underworld will carry the little ghost upon his shoulder because the boy is too little to walk so far. Is it not strange to find a Greek poet writing the very same thing thousands of years ago? The Greek poet was called Zonas of Sardis by some writers, by others he was called Diodorus,—his poem is addressed to the boatman who ferries the souls of men over the river of death.

"Do thou, who rowest the boat of the dead in the water of this lake full of reeds, for Hades, having a painful task to do, stretch out, dark Charon, thy hand to the son of Cinyrus, as he mounts on the ladder by the gangway, and receive him. *For his sandals will cause the lad to slip, and he fears to put his feet, naked, on the sands of the shore.*"

Again, just as it is the custom for little Japanese girls to make offerings of their dolls and toys to some divinity, in various parts of the country, so we find little Greek poems written to celebrate the doing of the same thing by Greek girls, ages before any modern European language had taken shape. The poet says in one of these, "Timarete has offered up her tambourine and her ball and her doll and her doll's dresses to thee, goddess, and do thou, O goddess, place thy hand over the girl and preserve her who thus devotes herself unto thee."

Hundreds of examples of this kind might be quoted. I mention them only by way of suggestion.

At the beginning of this lecture I remarked to you on the absence of poems about insects in the modern literature of the West. Of course, such absence means that the Western people have not yet perceived, much less understood, certain very beautiful sides of nature,—in spite of their study of the Greek poets. There may be reasons for this of another kind than you might at first suppose. It would not be just to say that Western people are deficient in aesthetic and ethical sensibility,—though they have not yet reached the Greek standard in that respect. It is not want of feeling; it is rather, I think, inability to consider nature in the largest and best way, because of the restraints that the Christian religion long placed upon Western thought. Christianity gave souls only to men,—not to animals or to insects. Familiarity with animals, however, compels men to recognise animal intelligence even while not daring to contradict the opinion of the Church.

Familiarity with insects, however, could not be obtained in the same way, nor have the like result. Even when men could recognise the spirit of a horse or the affectionate intelligence of a dog, they would still, under the influence of the old teaching, think only of insects as automata. In modern times, science has taught them better; but I am speaking of popular opinion. On the other hand, the philosophy of the Far East, teaching the unity of all life, would impel men to interest themselves in all living creatures,—just as did the Greek teaching that all forms of life had souls. One thing certainly strikes me as being very interesting. The few modern writers, in France and in England, who write about insect music, are men troubled by the mystery of the universe—men who have faced the great problems of oriental thought, and whose ears are therefore open to all the whispers of nature.

蟲にちなんだ仏蘭西の詩
Some French Poetry about Insects

Last year I gave a lecture on the subject of English poems about insects, with some reference to the old Greek poems on the same subject. But I did not then have an opportunity to make any reference to French poems upon the same subject, and I think that it would be a pity not to give you a few examples.

Just as in the case of English poems about insects, nearly all the French literature upon this subject is new. Insect poetry belongs to the newer and larger age of thought, to the age that begins to perceive the great truth of the unity of life. We no longer find, even in natural histories, the insect treated as a mere machine and unthinking organism; on the contrary its habits, its customs and its manifestation both of intelligence and instinct are being very carefully studied in these times, and a certain sympathy, as well as a certain feeling of respect or admiration, may be found in the scientific treatises of the greatest men who write about insect life. So, naturally, Europe is slowly returning to the poetical standpoint of the old Greeks in this respect. It is not improbable that keeping caged insects as pets may again become a Western custom, as it was in Greek times, when cages were made of rushes or straw for the little creatures. I suppose you have heard that the Japanese custom is very likely to become a fashion in America. If that should really happen, the fact would certainly have an effect upon poetry. I think that it is very likely to happen.

The French poets who have written pretty things about insects are nearly all poets of our own times. Some of them treat the subject from the old Greek standpoint—indeed the beautiful poem of Heredia upon the tomb of a grasshopper is perfectly Greek, and reads almost like a translation from the Greek. Other poets try to express the romance of insects in the form of a monologue, full of the thought of our own age. Others again touch the subject of insects only in connection with the subject of love. I will give one example of each method, keeping the best piece for the last, and beginning with a pretty fancy about a dragon-fly.

"Ma Libellule"

En te voyant toute mignonne,
Blanche dans ta robe d'azur,
Je pensais à quelque madone
Drapée en un peu de ciel pur;

Je songeais à ces belles saintes
Que l'on voyait, du temps jadis,
Sourire sur les vitres peintes,
Montrant d'un doigt le paradis;

Et j'aurais voulu, loin du monde
Qui passait frivole entre nous,
Dans quelque retraite profonde,
T'adorer seul à deux genoux.

This first part of the poem is addressed of course to a beautiful child, some girl between the age of childhood and womanhood:

"Beholding thee, Oh darling one, all white in thy azure dress, I thought of some figure of the Madonna robed in a shred of pure blue sky.

"I dreamed of those beautiful figures of saints whom one used to see in olden times smiling in the stained glass of church windows, and pointing upward to Paradise.

"And I could have wished to adore you alone upon my bended knees in some far hidden retreat, away from the frivolous world that passed between us."

This little bit of ecstasy over the beauty and purity of a child is pretty, but not particularly original. However, it is only an introduction. Now comes the pretty part of the poem:

Soudain, un caprice bizarre
Change la scène et le décor,
Et mon esprit au loin s'égare
Sur de grands prés d'azur et d'or,

Où, près de ruisseaux muscules,
Gazouillants comme des oiseaux,
Se poursuivent les libellules,
Ces fleurs vivantes des roseaux.

Enfant, n'es tu pas l'une d'elles
Qui poursuit pour me consoler?
Vainement tu caches tes ailes:
Tu marches, mais tu sais voler.

Petite fée au bleu corsage,
Que j'ai connu dès mon berceau,
En revoyant ton doux visage,
Je pense aux joncs de mon ruisseau!

Some French Poetry about Insects

Veux-tu qu'en amoureux fidèles
Nous revenions dans ces prés verts?
Libellule, reprends tes ailes,
Moi, je brûlerai tous mes vers!

Et nous irons, sous la lumière
D'un ciel plus frais et plus léger,
Chacun dans sa forme première,
Moi courir, et toi voltiger.

"Suddenly a strange fancy changes for me the scene and the scenery; and my mind wanders far away over great meadows of azure and gold.

"Where, hard by tiny streams that murmur with a sound like voices of little birds, the dragon-flies, those living flowers of the reeds, chase each other at play.

"Child, art thou not one of those dragon-flies, following after me to console me? Ah, it is in vain that thou tryest to hide thy wings; thou dost walk, indeed, but well thou knowest how to fly!

"O little fairy with the blue corsage whom I knew even from the time I was a baby in the cradle; seeing again thy sweet face, I think of the rushes that border the little stream of my native village!

"Dost thou not wish that even now as faithful lovers we return to those green fields? O dragon-fly, take thy wings again, and I—I will burn all my poetry,

"And we shall go back, under the light of the sky more fresh and pure than this, each of us in the original form—I to run about, and thou to hover in the air as of yore."

The sight of a child's face has revived for the poet very suddenly and vividly, the recollection of the village home, the green fields of childhood, the little stream where he used to play with the same little girl, sometimes running after the dragon-fly. And now the queer fancy comes to him that she herself is so like a dragon-fly—so light, graceful, spiritual! Perhaps really she is a dragon-fly following him into the great city, where he struggles to live as a poet, just in order to console him. She hides her wings, but that is only to prevent other people knowing. Why not return once more to the home of childhood, back to the green fields and the sun? "Little dragon-fly," he says to her, "let us go back! do you return to your beautiful summer shape, be a dragon-fly again, expand your wings of gauze; and I shall stop trying to write poetry. I shall burn my verses; I shall go back to the streams where we played as children; I shall run about again with the joy of a child, and with you beautifully flitting hither and thither as a dragon-fly."

Victor Hugo also has a little poem about a dragon-fly, symbolic only, but quite pretty. It is entitled "La Demoiselle"; and the other poem was entitled, as you remember, "Ma Libellule". Both words mean a dragon-fly, but not the same kind of dragon-fly. The French word "*demoiselle*", which might be adequately rendered into Japanese by the term *ojosan*, refers only to those exquisitely slender, graceful, slow-flitting dragon-flies known to the scientist by the name of Calopteryx. Of course you know the difference by sight, and the reason of the French name will be poetically apparent to you.

Quand la demoiselle dorée
S'envole au départ des hivers,
Souvent sa robe diaprée,
Souvent son aile est déchirée
Aux mille dards des buissons verts.

Ainsi, jeunesse vive et frêle,
Qui, t'égarant de tous côtés,

Some French Poetry about Insects

Voles où ton instinct t'appelle,
Souvent tu déchires ton aile
Aux épines des voluptés.

"When, at the departure of winter, the gilded dragon-fly begins to soar, often her many-coloured robe, often her wing, is torn by the thousand thorns of the verdant shrubs.

"Even so, O frail and joyous Youth, who, wandering hither and thither, in every direction, flyest wherever thy instinct calls thee—even so thou dost often tear thy wings upon the thorns of pleasure."

You must understand that pleasure is compared to a rose-bush, whose beautiful and fragrant flowers attract the insects, but whose thorns are dangerous to the visitors. However, Victor Hugo does not use the word for rose-bush, for obvious reasons; nor does he qualify the plants which are said to tear the wings of the dragon-fly. I need hardly tell you that the comparison would not hold good in reference to the attraction of flowers, because dragon-flies do not care in the least about flowers, and if they happen to tear their wings among thorn bushes, it is much more likely to be in their attempt to capture and devour other insects. The merit of the poem is chiefly in its music and colour; as natural history it would not bear criticism. The most beautiful modern French poem about insects, beautiful because of its classical perfection, is I think a sonnet by Heredia, entitled "Epigramme Funeraire"—that is to say, "Inscription for a Tombstone". This is an exact imitation of Greek sentiment and expression, carefully studied after the poets of the anthology. Several such Greek poems are extant, recounting how children mourned for pet insects which had died in spite of all their care. The most celebrated one among these I quoted in a former lecture—the poem about the little Greek girl

Myro who made a tomb for her grasshopper and cried over it. Heredia has very well copied the Greek feeling in this fine sonnet:

Ici gît, Étranger, la verte sauterelle
Que durant deux saisons nourrit la jeune Hellé,
Et dont l'aile vibrant sous le pied dentelé
Bruissait dans le pin, le cytise ou l'airelle.

Elle s'est tué, hélas! la lyre naturelle,
La muse des guérets, des sillons et du blé;
De peur que son léger sommeil ne soit troublé,
Ah! passe vite, ami, ne pèse point sur elle.

C'est là. Blanche, au milieu d'une touffe de thym,
Sa pierre funéraire est fraîchement posée.
Que d'hommes n'ont pas eu ce suprême destin!

Des larmes d'un enfant sa tombe est arrosée,
Et l'Aurore pieuse y fait chaque matin
Une libation de gouttes de rosée.

"Stranger, here reposes the green grasshopper that the young girl Helle cared for during two seasons,—the grasshopper whose wings, vibrating under the strokes of its serrated feet, used to resound in the pine, the trefoil and the whortleberry.

"She is silent now, alas! that natural lyre, muse of the unsown fields, of the furrows, and of the wheat. Lest her light sleep should be disturbed, ah! pass quickly, friend! do not be heavy upon her.

"It is there. All white, in the midst of a tuft of thyme, her funeral monument is placed, in cool shadow; how many men have not been able to have this supremely happy end!

Some French Poetry about Insects

"By the tears of a child the insect's tomb is watered; and the pious goddess of dawn each morning there makes a libation of drops of dew."

This reads very imperfectly in a hasty translation; the original charm is due to the perfect art of the form. But the whole thing, as I have said before, is really Greek, and based upon a close study of several little Greek poems on the same kind of subject. Little Greek girls thousands of years ago used to keep singing insects as pets, every day feeding them with slices of leek and with fresh water, putting in their little cages sprigs of the plants which they liked. The sorrow of the child for the inevitable death of her insect pets at the approach of winter, seems to have inspired many Greek poets. With all tenderness, the child would make a small grave for the insect, bury it solemnly, and put a little white stone above the place to imitate a grave-stone. But of course she would want an inscription for this tombstone—perhaps would ask some of her grown-up friends to compose one for her. Sometimes the grown-up friend might be a poet, in which case he would compose an epitaph for all time.

I suppose you perceive that the solemnity of this imitation of the Greek poems on the subject is only a tender mockery, a playful sympathy with the real grief of the child. The expression, "pass, friend", is often found in Greek funeral inscriptions together with the injunction to tread lightly upon the dust of the dead. There is one French word to which I will call attention,—the word "*guerets*". We have no English equivalent for this term, said to be a corruption of the Latin word "*veractum*", and meaning fields which have been ploughed but not sown.

Not to dwell longer upon the phase of art indicated by this poem, I may turn to the subject of crickets. There are many French poems about crickets. One by Lamartine is known to almost every French child.

Grillon, solitaire
Ici comme moi,
Voix qui sors de terre,
Ah! réveille-toi!
J'attise la flamme,
C'est pour t'égayer;
Mais il manque une âme
Une âme au foyer.

Grillon, solitaire
Voix qui sors de terre,
Ah! réveille-toi
Pour moi.

Quand j'étais petite
Comme ce berceau,
Et que Marguerite
Filait son fuseau,
Quand le vent d'automne
Faisait tout gémir,
Ton cri monotone
M'aidait à dormir.

Grillon, solitaire
Voix qui sors de terre,
Ah! réveille-toi
Pour moi.

Seize fois l'anné
A compté mes jeurs;
Dans la cheminée

Some French Poetry about Insects

Tu niches toujours.
Je t'écoute encore
Aux froides saisons,
Souvenir sonore
Des vieilles maisons.

Grillon, solitaire
Voix qui sors de terre,
Ah! réveille-toi
Pour moi.

It is a young girl who thus addresses the cricket of the hearth, the house cricket. It is very common in country houses in Europe. This is what she says:

"Little solitary cricket, all alone here just like myself, little voice that comes up out of the ground, ah, awake for my sake! I am stirring up the fires, that is just to make you comfortable; but there lacks a presence by the hearth; a soul to keep me company.

"When I was a very little girl, as little as that cradle in the corner of the room, then, while Margaret our servant sat there spinning, and while the autumn wind made everything moan outside, your monotonous cry used to help me to fall asleep.

"Solitary cricket, voice that issues from the ground, awaken, for my sake.

"Now I am sixteen years of age and you are still nestling in the chimneys as of old. I can hear you still in the cold season,—like a sound-memory,—a sonorous memory of old houses.

"Solitary cricket, voice that issues from the ground, awaken, O awaken for my sake."

I do not think this pretty little song needs any explanation; I would only call your attention to the natural truth of the fancy and the feeling. Sitting alone by the fire in the night, the maiden wants to hear the cricket sing, because it makes her think of her childhood, and she finds happiness in remembering it.

So far as mere art goes, the poem of Gautier on the cricket is very much finer than the poem of Lamartine, though not so natural and pleasing. But as Gautier was the greatest master of French verse in the nineteenth century, not excepting Victor Hugo, I think that one example of his poetry on insects may be of interest. He was very poor, compared with Victor Hugo; and he had to make his living by writing for newspapers, so that he had no time to become the great poet that nature intended him to be. However, he did find time to produce one volume of highly finished poetry, which is probably the most perfect verse of the nineteenth century, if not the most perfect verse ever made by a French poet; I mean the "Émaux et Camées". But the little poem which I am going to read to you is not from the "Émaux et Camées".

Souffle, bise! tombe à flots, pluie!
Dans mon palais, tout noir de suie,
Je ris de la pluie et du vent;
En attendant que l'hiver fuie,
Je reste au coin du feu, rêvant.

C'est moi qui suis l'esprit de l'âtre!
Le gaz, de sa langue bleuâtre,
Lèche plus doucement le bois;
La fumée, en filet d'albâtre,
Monte et se contourne à ma voix.

La bouilloire rit et babille;
La flamme aux pieds d'argent sautille

Some French Poetry about Insects

En accompagnant ma chanson;
La bûche de duvet s'habille;
La sève bout dans le tison.

* * * * *

Pendant la nuit et la journée
Je chante sous la cheminée;
Dans mon langage de grillon
J'ai, des rebuts de son aînée,
Souvent consolé Cendrillon.

* * * * *

Quel plaisir! Prolonger sa veille,
Regarder la flamme vermeille
Prenant à deux bras le tison;
A tous les bruits prêter l'oreille;
Entendre vivre la maison!

Tapi dans sa niche bien chaude,
Sentir l'hiver qui pleure et rôde,
Tout blême et le nez violet,
Tâchant de s'introduire en fraude
Par quelque fente du volet.

This poem is especially picturesque, and is intended to give us the comfortable sensations of a winter night by the fire, and the amusement of watching the wood burn and of hearing the kettle boiling. You will find that the French has a particular quality of lucid expression; it is full of clearness and colour.

"Blow on, cold wind! pour down, O rain. I, in my soot-black palace, laugh at both rain and wind; and while waiting for winter to pass I remain in my corner by the fire dreaming.

"It is I that am really the spirit of the hearth! The gaseous flame licks the wood more softly with its bluish tongue when it hears me; and the smoke rises up like an alabaster thread, and curls itself about (or twists) at the sound of my voice.

"The kettle chuckles and chatters; the golden-footed flame leaps, dancing to the accompaniment of my song (or in accompaniment to my song); the great log covers itself with down, the sap boils in the wooden embers ("*duvet*", meaning "down", refers to the soft fluffy white ash that forms upon the surface of burning wood).

"All night and all day I sing below the chimney. Often in my cricket-language, I have consoled Cinderella for the snubs of her elder sister.

"Ah, what pleasure to sit up at night, and watch the crimson flames embracing the wood (or hugging the wood) with both arms at once, and to listen to all the sounds and to hear the life of the house!

"Nestling in one's good warm nook, how pleasant to hear Winter, who weeps and prowls round about the house outside, all wan and blue-nosed with cold, trying to smuggle itself inside some chink in the shutter!"

Of course this does not give us much about the insect itself, which remains invisible in the poem, just as it really remains invisible in the house where the voice is heard. Rather does the poem express the feelings of the person who hears the cricket.

When we come to the subject of grasshoppers, I think that the French poets have done much better than the English. There are many poems on the field grasshopper; I scarcely know which to quote first. But I think you would be pleased with a little composition by the celebrated

Some French Poetry about Insects

French painter, Jules Breton. Like Rossetti he was both painter and poet; and in both arts he took for his subjects by preference things from country life. This little poem is entitled "Les Cigales". The word "*cigales*", though really identical with our word "*cicala*", seldom means the same thing. Indeed the French word may mean several different kinds of insects, and it is only by studying the text that we can feel quite sure what sort of insect is meant.

Lorsque dans l'herbe mûre aucun épi ne bouge,
Qu'à l'ardeur des rayons crépite le froment,
Que le coquelicot tombe languissamment
Sous le faible fardeau de sa corolle rouge,

Tous les oiseaux de l'air ont fait taire leurs chants;
Les ramiers paresseux, au plus noir des ramures,
Somnolents, dans les bois, ont cessé leurs murmures,
Loin du soleil muet incendiant les champs.

Dans le blé, cependant, d'intrépides cigales
Jetant leurs mille bruits, fanfare de l'été,
Ont frénétiquement et sans trêve agité
Leurs ailes sur l'airain de leurs folles cymbales.

Trémoussantes, deboutes sur les longs épis d'or,
Virtuoses qui vont s'éteindre avant l'automne,
Elles poussent au ciel leur hymne monotone,
Qui dans l'ombre des nuits retentissait encore.

Et rien n'arrêtera leurs cris intarissables;
Quand on les chassera de l'avoine et des blés,
Elles émigreront sur les buissons brûlés
Qui se meurent de soif dans les déserts de sables.

Sur l'arbuste effeuillé, sur les chardons flétris
Qui laissent s'envoler leur blanche chevelure,
On reverra l'insecte à la forte encolure.
Pleine d'ivresse, toujours s'exalter dans ses cris.

Jusqu'à ce qu'ouvrant l'aile en lambeaux arrachée,
Exaspéré, brûlant d'un feu toujours plus pur,
Son œil de bronze fixe et tendu vers l'azur,
Il expire en chantant sur la tige séchée.

For the word "*encolure*" we have no English equivalent; it means the line of the neck and shoulder—sometimes the general appearance of shape of the body.

"When in the ripening grain field not a single ear of wheat moves; when in the beaming heat the corn seems to crackle; when the poppy languishes and bends down under the feeble burden of its scarlet corolla,

"Then all the birds of the air have hushed their songs; even the indolent doves, seeking the darkest part of the foliage in the tree, have become drowsy in the woods, and have ceased their cooing, far from the fields, which the silent sun is burning.

"Nevertheless, in the wheat, the brave grasshoppers uttering their thousand sounds, a trumpet flourish of summer, have continued furiously and unceasingly to smite their wings upon the brass of their wild cymbal.

"Quivering as they stand upon the long gold ears of the grain, master musicians who must die before the coming of Fall, they sound to heaven their monotonous hymn, which re-echoes even in the darkness of the night.

"And nothing will check their inexhaustible shrilling. When chased away from the oats and from the wheat, they will migrate to the scorched bushes which die of thirst in the wastes of sand.

Some French Poetry about Insects

"Upon the leafless shrubs, upon the dried up thistles, which let their white hair fall and float away, there the sturdily-built insect can be seen again, filled with enthusiasm, even more and more excited as he cries,

"Until, at last, opening his wings, now rent into shreds, exasperated, burning more and more fiercely in the frenzy of his excitement, and with his eyes of bronze always fixed motionlessly upon the azure sky, he dies in his song upon the withered grain."

This is difficult to translate at all satisfactorily, owing to the multitude of images compressed together. But the idea expressed is a fine one—the courage of the insect challenging the sun, and only chanting more and more as the heat and the thirst increase. The poem has, if you like, the fault of exaggeration, but the colour and music are very fine; and even the exaggeration itself has the merit of making the images more vivid.

It will not be necessary to quote another text; we shall scarcely have the time; but I want to translate to you something of another poem upon the same insect by the modern French poet Jean Aicard. In this poem, as in the little poem by Gautier, which I quoted to you, the writer puts his thought in the mouth of the insect, so to say—that is, makes the insect tell its own story.

"I am the impassive and noble insect that sings in the summer solstice from the dazzling dawn all the day long in the fragrant pine-wood. And my song is always the same, regular as the equal course of the season and of the sun. I am the speech of the hot and beaming sun, and when the reapers, weary of heaping the sheaves together, lie down in the lukewarm shade, and sleep and pant in the ardour of noonday—then more than at any other time do I utter freely and joyously that double-echoing strophe with which my whole body vibrates. And when nothing else moves in all the land round about, I palpitate and loudly sound my little drum. Otherwise the sunlight triumphs; and in the whole landscape nothing is heard but my cry,— like the joy of the light itself.

"Like a butterfly I take up from the hearts of the flowers that pure water which the night lets fall into them like tears. I am inspired only by the almighty sun. Socrates listened to me; Virgil made mention of me. I am the insect especially beloved by the poets and by the bards. The ardent sun reflects himself in the globes of my eyes. My ruddy bed, which seems to be powdered like the surface of fine ripe fruit, resembles some exquisite key-board of silver and gold, all quivering with music. My four wings, with their delicate net-work of nerves, allow the bright down upon my black back to be seen through their transparency. And like a star upon the forehead of some divinely inspired poet, three exquisitely mounted rubies glitter upon my head."

These are fair examples of the French manner of treating the interesting subject of insects in poetry. If you should ask me whether the French poets are better than the English, I should answer, "In point of feeling, no." The real value of such examples to the student should be emotional, not descriptive. I think that the Japanese poems on insects, though not comparable in point of mere form with some of the foreign poems which I have quoted, are better in another way—they come nearer to the true essence of poetry. For the Japanese poets have taken the subject of insects chiefly for the purpose of suggesting human emotion; and that is certainly the way in which such a subject should be used. Remember that this is an age in which we are beginning to learn things about insects which could not have been even imagined fifty years ago, and the more that we learn about these miraculous creatures, the more dif-

Some French Poetry about Insects

ficult does it become for us to write poetically about their lives, or about their possible ways of thinking and feeling. Probably no mortal man will ever be able to imagine how insects think or feel or hear or even see. Not only are their senses totally different from those of animals, but they appear to have a variety of special senses about which we can not know anything at all. As for their existence, it is full of facts so atrocious and so horrible as to realise most of the imaginations of old about the torments of hell. Now, for these reasons to make an insect speak in poetry—to put one's thoughts, so to speak, into the mouth of an insect—is no longer consistent with poetical good judgment. No; we must think of insects either in relation to the mystery of their marvellous lives, or in relation to the emotion which their sweet and melancholy music makes within our minds. The impressions produced by hearing the shrilling of crickets at night or by hearing the storm of cicadae in summer woods—those impressions indeed are admirable subjects for poetry, and will continue to be for all time.

When I lectured to you long ago about Greek and English poems on insects, I told you that nearly all the English poems on the subject were quite modern. I still believe that I was right in this statement, as a general assertion; but I have found one quaint poem about a grasshopper, which must have been written about the middle of the seventeenth century or, perhaps, a little earlier. The date of the author's birth and death are respectively 1618 and 1658. His name, I think, you are familiar with—Richard Lovelace, author of many amatory poems, and of one especially famous song, "To Lucasta, on Going to the Wars"—containing the celebrated stanza—

Yet this inconstancy is such
As you too shall adore;

I could not love thee, Dear, so much,
Loved I not honour more.

Well, as I said, this man wrote one pretty little poem on a grasshopper, which antedates most of the English poems on insects, if not all of them.

"The Grasshopper"

O Thou that swing'st upon the waving ear
Of some well-filled oaten beard,
Drunk every night with a delicious tear
Dropt thee from heaven, where now th'art rear'd!

The joys of earth and air are thine entire,
That with thy feet and wings dost hop and fly;
And when thy poppy works, thou dost retire
To thy carved acorn-bed to lie.

Up with the day, the Sun thou welcom'st then,
Sport'st in the gilt plaits of his beams,
And all these merry days mak'st merry men
Thyself, and melancholy streams.

A little artificial, this poem written at least two hundred and fifty years ago; but it is pretty in spite of its artifice. Some of the conceits are so quaint that they must be explained. By the term "oaten beard", the poet means an ear of oats; and you know that the grain of this plant is furnished with very long hair, so that many poets have spoken of the bearded oats. You may remember in this connection Tennyson's phrase "the bearded barley" in the "Lady of Shalott", and Longfellow's term "bearded grain" in his famous poem about the Reaper Death. When a person's beard is very thick, we say in England to-day "a full beard", but in the time of Shakespeare they used to say "a well filled beard"—hence the phrase in the second line of the first stanza.

In the third line the term "delicious tear" means—dew,—which the Greeks called the tears of the night, and sometimes the tears of the dawn; and the phrase "drunk with dew" is quite Greek—so we may suspect that the author of this poem had been reading the Greek Anthology. In the third line of the second stanza the word "poppy" is used for sleep—a very common simile in Elizabethan times, because from the poppy flower was extracted the opiate which enables sick persons to sleep. The Greek authors spoke of poppy sleep. "And when thy poppy works", means, when the essence of sleep begins to operate upon you, or more simply, when you sleep. Perhaps the phrase about the "carved acorn-bed" may puzzle you; it is borrowed from the fairy-lore of Shakespeare's time, when fairies were said to sleep in little beds carved out of acorn shells; the simile is used only by way of calling the insect a fairy creature. In the second line of the third stanza you may notice the curious expression about the "gilt plaits" of the sun's beams. It was the custom in those days, as it still is in these, for young girls to plait their long hair; and the expression "gilt plaits" only means braided or plaited golden hair. This is perhaps a Greek conceit; for classic poets spoke of the golden hair of the Sun God as illuminating the world. I have said that the poem is a little artificial, but I think you will find it pretty, and even the whimsical similes are "precious" in the best sense.

昆蟲の政治学
Insect Politics

A leading New York daily has a delightful editorial upon "Communism among Ants". That ants have a civilisation has been known for a long time. And naturalists never weary of studying the government of their little communities. They have an architecture, less mathematically beautiful, perhaps, than that of the bees, but more varied, and more wonderful. Their builders construct subterranean cities wonderful as the labyrinths of Egypt according to Herodotus; palaces as fragile and delicate as the residences of the Oriental Caliphs, and the military fortifications worthy of French engineers. The African white ants erect domed structures sometimes eight and ten feet in height and even higher, with minarets like those of a Turkish mosque, and so strongly built as to bear the weight of a heavy man on their summits. The red and black ants make fierce war, advancing to the attack in columns and companies. They go on slaving expeditions, and capture myriads of aphidae—the beautiful green parasites which love the juicy geranium. These they feed and milk like cattle. But latterly the discovery has been made that their political system is occasionally disturbed by socialistic agitators. Certain ants who hoard too much golden honey, or other wealth, are occasionally the victims of communistic riots. The poor and starving ants strike against the tyranny of capital, slay the millionaires,

Insect Politics

and distribute their hoards throughout the community. So that there are more things to be learned from the ant than Solomon ever dreamed of.

街燈の下にて
Under the Electric Light

A sound as of the boiling of a prodigious pot, the bubbling of a witches' cauldron, under the electric light. Such was the music of the insect orchestra at the West End last evening.

It was worth the price of the trip alone to behold the spectacle,—a veritable realisation of the swarm of flies that afflicted the land of Egypt.

The insects hung about the lights like thin clouds above the face of the moon. The sky was actually obscured at intervals. But the little creatures did not bite. They only uttered their wailing music, and formed a living canopy above the heads of the people, like the canopy formed by the enchanted birds above the head of Soliman in Arabic tradition.

They entered Micholet's restaurant uninvited, and pounced like Harpies upon the viands, soiling what they could not carry away.

Whether the wind brought them or the lights of the music, we can not positively say; but at ten o'clock they positively disappeared as if by magic.

It seems not improbable that the electric lights exercise a certain fascination upon them, and perhaps also the sound of music; for mosquitoes have a fine ear for harmony.

At all events they came to the fort together with the crowd of human visitors, and thinned away as the people began to withdraw, after having enjoyed the evening as much as anybody, and secured all the privileges and pleasures and luxuries of the resort without paying therefor. The phenomenon was certainly a most curious one.

——!——!! 蚊!!!
——!——!! *Mosquitoes!!!*

The mosquito is the most cunning of all living things which fly. She sees by night even better than by day. She knows by heart all the holes in every mosquito curtain in the largest hotels. She is a first class judge of dry goods, and distinguishes afar off the quality and thickness of socks and stockings. She poketh her little bill through the finest material that modern machinery can spin.

We say "she" because our tormenters are females; the male mosquitoes are respectable, well behaved boys who remain where they are born. Only feminine malice can explain the ingenious capacity for torment possessed by the mosquito which plays vampire both by night and by day.

When a mosquito lights softly with a subdued scream of triumph on the end of your nose, or any other end, she always keeps one leg hoisted high in air, so as to be ready to flee at a moment's notice. It is only when she puts that leg down that you have any chance of ending her pernicious existence.

Another matter in which biting mosquitoes show their feminine characteristics is their dislike of tobacco.

But they also possess feminine patience, and will wait hours for a smoker to finish his pipe. Then they will take ample revenge.

Nevertheless mosquitoes have their users.

——! ——!! *Mosquitoes!!!*

If it were not for mosquitoes we should all become terribly lazy in this climate. We should waste our time snoring upon sofas or lolling in easy chairs, or gossiping about trivial things, or dreaming vain dreams, or longing after things which belong to our neighbours, or feeling dissatisfied with our lot, instead of humping ourselves and scooting around and making money. Idleness is the mother of all vices; and mosquitoes know this as well as anybody, and not being lazy themselves they will not suffer us to be lazy.

It is for this reason that they hum around only in summer when everything is lazy and drowsy,—especially on one of those quiet summer days when everything is so silent that one can hear the cocks crowing to each other at long distances, and answering each other like sentries in the old cities of Spanish-America. For in winter time the cold forces us to make ourselves useful as well as ornamental.

And so, even while we curse, let us also bless the mosquitoes, for making us move about and root around, instead of dreaming our lives away.

祭りを想わせて
The Festive

He maketh ghostly noises in the dead waste and middle of the night.

He hath a passion for the green and crimson of beautifully bound books, and after he has passed over them they look as if they has been sprinkled with vitriol.

He loveth to commit suicide by drowning himself in bowls of cream or stifling himself in other eatables or drinkables.

When trod upon he explodeth with a great noise.

In this semi-tropical climate he sometimes attaineth to the dimensions of a No. 12 shoe.

He haunteth printing offices, and fatteneth upon the contents of the editor's paste-pot, and upon the bindings of newspaper files.

He haunteth kitchens and occasionally getteth himself baked and boiled.

Five hundred thousand means have been invented for his destruction; but none availeth.

If a house be burnt down to the ground, he will momentarily disappear; but when the house is rebuilt, he cometh back again.

His virtues are these: He amuseth young kittens, who practice mouse-hunting with them. Also he is the deadly enemy of the *Cimex lectularius*. He is used for medicinal purposes.

The Festive

But none care to recognise his good qualities, because of the mischievous and disgusting propensities, and all creatures wage unrelenting war against him, and nevertheless he continueth to propagate his species and to drown himself in cream.

玉蟲
The Jewel Insect

The Jewel Insect was so pretty that all the other handsome insects wanted to marry her. Every day many butterflies and moths and gnats and other creatures came to her house, and said to her: "I love you very much; please be my wife!"

Now the Jewel Insect could not marry any one of them. But she did not like to tell them so. She was afraid that they would get angry with her. So she was cunning with them, and said to them: "I will marry the first of you who brings me some pretty fire. But remember, it must be really pretty fire, and not cold, like the fire of the fire-flies."

They all flew away to get fire for her. But they never came back again. The pretty fire burned them up. And that is why on summer nights, so many insects burn themselves in Mama's lamp.

ハバー氏の大欄蜘蛛
Dr. Hava's Tarantula

Dr. Hava contributes to the last *Comptes-rendus de l'Athénée Louisianais* a really delightful little paper upon certain venomous insects of the tropics—especially in Tarantula. When quite a little boy in Cuba he pursued entomology in a scientific fashion; and certainly that wonderful island affords admirable opportunities for studies of this kind. Naturally these juvenile studies were not without their drawbacks; and the writers gives us quite an amusing history of one of his first efforts in this direction. He has long been anxious to capture a specimen of a certain hymenopterous insect called in Cuba "the Devil's Horse",—in other words a species of gigantic wasp or hornet as large as a humming bird. One day he managed to capture the Devil's Horse by throwing his hat over it; and what followed we had better let him tell in his own words:

—"I committed a great imprudence; I clapped my hat upon my head with the Devil's Horse in it; and then it was I discovered for the first time in my life that there is no complete happiness in this world. The creature pierced my scalp with his terrible sting. And although at that time I possessed a very abundant head of hair, in spite of the thick covering of my dishevelled mane, I came home all exhausted, dizzy and suffering, although triumphant and at full gallop—not I upon the Devil's Horse but the Devil's Horse upon me . . . When my grandmother saw the creature entangled in my hair; she armed herself with a large napkin and snatched him off my head so quickly that he flew away before I could even turn around to catch him again. Under the weight of this disappointment I began to cry and find fault with my grandmother for being so awkward; but this trouble soon yielded to sharp pains in my head and a terrible swelling, which I could feel momentarily increasing. All my head, neck, and face—more especially my eyelids, become greatly swelled; I had received a terrible urtication, but in a few hours this disappeared under the influence of cool lotions, slightly alkaline."

By the way, some of our readers must remember Dr. Hava's rattlesnake, which appeared to live in harmony with a mouse, and used daily to attract a crowd before the Doctor's drugstore window. The SPCA ordered the Doctor to release the mouse and "free the serpent".

"I yielded at once," ironically observed the Doctor; "and giving the key of the cage to the good man, told him to execute the philanthropic order himself; but the employee refused under the pretext that it was not his duty to do such things. It is hardly necessary to observe that after this act of submission on my part, no one ever came to me afterwards with the same pretensions. Now it came to pass one day that the serpent happened to disturb the slumbers of his majesty the mouse and the little animal actually had the courage to bite the serpent on the head. You may feel assured that so polite a serpent could not partially endure such a violation of his laws of hospitality. It was a gross insult, in avenging which he would have been justified by the most humanitarian laws, even though he had killed his best friend."

The main portion of Dr. Hava's article, however, is devoted to the study of the Tarantula, a remarkably fine specimen of which he had recently an exhibition at his drug store on Chartres Street. In connection with a little dissertation on the effects of the venom of this gigantic spider and other tropical monsters, the Doctor relates the following pretty account of a curious personal experience.

—"I was passing one day before a house where some of my intimate friends lived, and there was a sudden cry for help. A young, beautiful, white-and-ruddy girl had just screamed and fainted. I rushed in, opened the girl's corsage and found that a scorpion had bitten her between the breasts. Fortunately it had only bitten her once. After removing and crushing the reptile, I sucked the wound until I felt certain that I had extracted all venom; and it healed without any evil consequences . . . It is said that the Romans when stung by vipers used to have the wounds sucked by slaves who succumbed to the poison immediately after having saved the lives of their masters. This is false; venoms act solely upon the blood; and I myself who actually played the part of the Roman slave preserve only a pleasant memory of this accomplishment of duty."

But to return to the tarantula, *Lyosa tarantula*, which takes its name from the city of Taranto, in the South of Italy. There was an epidemic disorder called tarantism, which prevailed for a long time in Italy during the Middle Ages, and was said to have been produced by the bite of spiders of this species. The victims of tarantism danced until exhausted, after which they would take a sea bath with curative results. This epidemic is now believed to have been caused by nothing more than the nervous and mental disorders which prevailed throughout Europe in that period. The author of *Epidemics of the Middle Ages* has preserved in his curious work the music of the famous "Tarantula Dance".

Dr. Hava mentions that the bite of the tarantula produces none of these "choreographic effects", although highly dangerous. Loss of speech for even six months, may occur in consequences of it;—the Doctor mentions such a case.

The tarantula spins no web; but secretes a sort of viscous plaster in her abdomen of a similar nature to that used by other spiders—(there are more than 3,000 different kinds of arachnida)—in spinning; with this she makes her nest, screens herself from the light, and defends her little ones from their natural enemies.

Among the greatest enemies of spiders are wasps; and their wars are of ghastliness unutterable. The wasp conquers almost inevitably—just as the falcon or owl vanquishes its prey. But the purpose and work of the wasp in her attack are wholly different. The wasp circles above and about the spider as an eagle above a snake, until she gets a chance to sting. The sting paralyses the spider; and the wasp lays her eggs in the victim's body. For eighty long days the wretched spider lives as in a nightmare, unable to move, with entrails devoured by the larvae of the wasp. The larvae become pupae; and pupae wasps, which issue from their living home in the full glory of yellow and black mail and crystal wing. Then and only then the wretched spider dies.

This fact accounts for the torpid siders so often found in wasps' nests, whither they are carried for the purpose above referred to.

Now the enemy of the tarantula, the largest of the spiders, is "the Devil's Horse" above referred to,—the largest of wasps. We say the largest of spiders, on the authority of Dr. Hava; for although we have seen Indian species larger than a dozen American tarantulas put together, we suppose they are only another variety of the same creature, like those monstrous living spiders of the Asiatic steppes, as large as a man's two fists. Probably these two have en-

Dr. Hava's Tarantula

emies in the shape of proportionally large wasps. After the Devil's Horse, (or rather the Devil's Mare, for it is the female wasp who perpetrates these horrors), has stung the tarantula, she drags the paralysed victim to a hiding place, and deposits her eggs in the spider's living substance; and the Doctor truly observes that all the tortures ever inflicted upon human beings for the sake of religion or vengeance or superstition, all the atrocities perpetrated by Oriental despots or Chinese tyrants,—all the cruelties recorded in the *Dictionaire de la Pénalité*—pale beside the penalty of defeat which the tarantula suffers.

餓鬼
Gaki

—*"Venerable Nagasena, are there such things as demons in the world?"*
—*"Yes, O King."*
—*"Do they ever leave that condition of existence?"*
—*"Yes, they do."*
—*"But, if so, why is it that the remains of those demons are never found?"*
—*"Their remains are found, O King . . . The remains of bad demons can be found in the form of worms and beetles and ants and snakes and scorpions and centipedes."*

– The Questions of King Milinda

I.

There are moments in life when truths but dimly known before—beliefs first vaguely reached through multiple processes of reasoning—suddenly assume the vivid character of emotional convictions. Such an experience came to me the other day, on the Suruga coast. While resting under the pines that fringed the beach, something in the vital warmth and luminous peace of the hour—some quivering rapture of wind and light—very strangely bestirred an old belief of mine: the belief that all being is One. One I felt myself to be with

the thrilling of breeze and the racing of wave—with every flutter of shadow and flicker of sun—with the azure of sky and sea—with the great green hush of the land. In some new and wonderful way I found myself assured that there never could have been a beginning—that there never could be an end. Nevertheless, the ideas of the moment were not new: the novelty of the experience was altogether in the peculiar intensity with which they presented themselves; making me feel that the flashing dragon-flies, and the long grey sand-crickets, and the shrilling *sémi* overhead, and the little red crabs astir under the roots of the pines, were all of them brothers and sisters. I seemed to understand, as never before, how the mystery that is called the Soul of me must have quickened in every form of past existence, and must as certainly continue to behold the sun, for other millions of summers, through eyes of other countless shapes of future being. And I tried to think the long slow thoughts of the long grey crickets—and the thoughts of the darting, shimmering dragon-flies—and the thoughts of the basking, trilling cicadae—and the thoughts of the wicked little crabs that lifted up their claws from between the roots of the pines.

Presently I discovered myself wondering whether the consequence of such thoughts could have anything to do with the recombination of my soul-dust in future spheres of existence. For thousands of years the East has been teaching that what we think or do in this life really decides— through some inevitable formation of atom-tendencies, or polarities—the future place of our substance, and the future state of our sentiency. And the belief is worth thinking about—though no amount of thinking can enable us either to confirm or to disprove it. Very possibly, like other Buddhist doctrines, it may adumbrate some cosmic truth; but its literal assertions I doubt, because I must doubt the

Gaki

power ascribed to thought. By the whole infinite past I have been moulded, within and without: how should the impulse of a moment reshape me against the weight of the eternities? . . . Buddhism indeed answers how, and that astounding answer is irrefutable—but I doubt . . .

Anyhow, acts and thoughts, according to Buddhist doctrine, are creative. Visible matter is made by acts and thoughts—even the universe of stars, and all that has form and name, and all the conditions of existence. What we think or do is never for the moment only, but for measureless time: it signifies some force directed to the shaping of worlds—to the making of future bliss or pain. Remembering this, we may raise ourselves to the zones of the Gods. Ignoring it, we may deprive ourselves even of the right to be reborn among men, and may doom ourselves, though innocent of the crimes that cause rebirth in hell, to re-enter existence in the form of animals, or of insects, or of goblins—gaki.[1]

So it depends upon ourselves whether we are to become insects or goblins hereafter; and in the Buddhist system the difference between insects and goblins is not so well defined as might be supposed. The belief in a mysterious relation between ghosts and insects, or rather between spirits and insects, is a very ancient belief in the East, where it now assumes innumerable forms—some unspeakably horrible, others full of weird beauty. "The White Moth" of Mr. Quiller-Couch would not impress a Japanese reader as novel; for the night-moth or the butterfly figures in many a Japanese poem and legend as the soul of a lost wife. The night-cricket's thin lament is perhaps the sorrowing of a voice once human;—the strange red marks upon the heads of cicadae are characters of spirit-names;—dragon-flies and grasshoppers are the horses of the dead. All these are to be pitied with the pity that is kin to love. But the noxious and dangerous insects represent the results of another quality of Karma that which produces goblins and demons. Grisly names have been given to some of these insects—as, for example, "*Jigokumushi*", or "Hell-Insect", to the ant-lion; and "*Kappa-mushi*", to a gigantic water-beetle which seizes frogs and fish, and devours them alive, thus realising, in a microcosmic way, the hideous myth of the Kappa, or River-Goblin. Flies, on the other hand, are especially identified with the world of hungry ghosts. How often, in the season of flies, have I heard some persecuted toiler exclaim, "*Kyō no hai wa, gaki no yo da nê?*" (The flies to-day, how like gaki they are!)

II.

In the old Japanese, or, more correctly speaking, Chinese, Buddhist literature relating to the gaki, the Sanscrit names of the gaki are given in a majority of cases; but some classes of gaki described have only Chinese names. As the Indian belief reached Japan by way of China and Korea, it is likely to have received a peculiar colouring in the course of its journey. But, in a general way, the Japanese classification of gaki corresponds closely to the Indian classification of the *pretas*.

The place of gaki in the Buddhist system is but one degree removed from the region of the hells, or Jigokudō—the lowest of all the States of Existence. Above the Jigokudō is the Gakidō, or World of Hungry Spirits; above the Gakidō is the Chikushōdō, or World of Animals; and above this, again, is the Shuradō, a region of perpetual fighting and slaughter. Higher than these is placed the Ningendō, or World of Mankind.

Now a person released from hell, by exhaustion of the Karma that sent him there, is seldom reborn at once into

Gaki

the zone of human existence, but must patiently work his way upward thither, through all the intermediate states of being. Many of the gaki have been in hell.

But there are gaki also who have not been in hell. Certain kinds or degrees of sin may cause a person to be reborn as a gaki immediately after having died in this world. Only the greatest degree of sin condemns the sinner directly to hell. The second degree degrades him to the Gakidō. The third causes him to be reborn as an animal.

Japanese Buddhism recognises thirty-six principal classes of gaki. "Roughly counting," says the *Shōbō-nen-jō-kyō*, "we find thirty-six classes of gaki; but should we attempt to distinguish all the different varieties, we should find them to be innumerable." The thirty-six classes form two great divisions, or orders. One comprises all "Gaki-World-Dwellers" (*Gaki-Sekai-Jū*);—that is to say, all Hungry Spirits who remain in the Gakidō proper, and are, therefore, never seen by mankind. The other division is called "*Nin-chū-Jū*", or "Dwellers among men": these gaki remain always in this world, and are sometimes seen.

There is yet another classification of gaki, according to the character of their penitential torment. All gaki suffer hunger and thirst; but there are three degrees of this suffering. The *Muzai-gaki* represent the first degree: they must hunger and thirst uninterruptedly, without obtaining any nourishment whatever. The *Shōzai-gaki* suffer only in the second degree: they are able to feed occasionally upon impure substances. The *Usai-gaki* are more fortunate: they can eat such remains of food as are thrown away by men, and also the offerings of food set before the images of the gods, or before the tablets of the ancestors. The last two classes of gaki are especially interesting, because they are supposed to meddle with human affairs.

Insect Literature

Before modern science introduced exact knowledge of the nature and cause of certain diseases, Buddhists explained the symptoms of such diseases by the hypothesis of gaki. Certain kinds of intermittent fever, for example, were said to be caused by a gaki entering the human body for the sake of nourishment and warmth. At first the patient would shiver with cold, because the gaki was cold. Then, as the gaki gradually became warm, the chill would pass, to be succeeded by a burning heat. At last the satiated haunter would go away, and the fever disappear; but upon another day, and usually at an hour corresponding to that of the first attack, a second fit of ague would announce the return of the gaki. Other zymotic disorders could be equally well explained as due to the action of gaki.

In the *Shōbō-nen-jō-kyō* a majority of the thirty-six kinds of gaki are associated with putrescence, disease, and death. Others are plainly identified with insects. No particular kind of gaki is identified by name with any particular kind of insect; but the descriptions suggest conditions of insect-life; and such suggestions are re-enforced by a knowledge of popular superstitions. Perhaps the descriptions are vague in the case of such spirits as the *Jiki-ketsu-gaki*, or blood-suckers; the *Jiki-niku-gaki*, or flesh-eaters; the *Jiki-da-gaki*, or ****-eaters; the Jiki-fun-gaki, or ****-eaters; the *Jiki-doku-gaki*, or poison-eaters; the *Jiki-fu-gaki*, or wind-eaters; the *Jiki-ké-gaki*, or smell-eaters; the *Jiki-kwa-gaki*, or fire-eaters (perhaps they fly into lamps?); the *Shikkō-gaki*, who devour corpses and cause pestilence; the *Shinen-gaki*, who appear by night as wandering fires; the *Shin-ko-gaki*, or needle-mouthed; and the Kwaku-shin-ga-ki, or cauldron-bodied—each a living furnace, filled with flame that keeps the fluids of its body humming like a boiling pot. But the suggestion of the following excerpts[2] will not be found at all obscure:

Gaki

"*Jiki-man-gaki.*—These gaki can live only by eating the wigs of false hair with which the statues of certain divinities are decorated . . . Such will be the future condition of persons who steal objects of value from Buddhist temples.

"*Fujō-ko-hyaku-gaki.*—These gaki can eat only street filth and refuse. Such a condition is the consequence of having given putrid or unwholesome food to priests or nuns, or pilgrims in need of alms.

"*Cho-ken-jū-jiki-netsu-gaki.*—These are the eaters of the refuse of funeral-pyres and of the clay of graves . . . They are the spirits of men who despoiled Buddhist temples for the sake of gain.

"*Ju-chū-gaki.*—These spirits are born within the wood of trees, and are tormented by the growing of the grain . . . Their condition is the result of having cut down shade-trees for the purpose of selling the timber. Persons who cut down the trees in Buddhist cemeteries or temple-grounds are especially likely to become *ju-chū-gaki.*"[3]

Moths, flies, beetles, grubs, worms, and other unpleasant creatures seem thus to be indicated. But some kinds of gaki cannot be identified with insects—for example, the species called *Jiki-hō-gaki*, or doctrine-eaters. These can exist only by hearing the preaching of the Law of the Buddha in some temple. While they hear such preaching, their torment is assuaged; but at all other times they suffer agonies unspeakable. To this condition are liable after death all Buddhist priests or nuns who proclaim the law for the mere purpose of making money . . . Also there are gaki who appear sometimes in beautiful human shapes. Such are the *Yoku-shiki-gaki*, spirits of lewdness—corresponding in some sort to the incubi and succubi of our own Middle Ages. They can change their sex at will, and can make their bodies as large or as small as they please. It

Insect Literature

is impossible to exclude them from any dwelling, except by the use of holy charms and spells, since they are able to pass through an orifice even smaller than the eye of a needle. To seduce young men, they assume beautiful feminine shapes—often appearing at wine-parties as waitresses or dancing girls.

To seduce women they take the form of handsome lads. This state of *Yoku-shiki-gaki* is a consequence of lust in some previous human existence; but the supernatural powers belonging to their condition are results of meritorious Karma which the evil Karma could not wholly counterbalance.

Even concerning the *Yoku-shiki-gaki*, however, it is plainly stated that they may take the form of insects. Though wont to appear in human shape, they can assume the shape of any animal or other creature, and "fly freely in all directions of space"—or keep their bodies "so small that mankind cannot see them." . . . All insects are not necessarily gaki; but most gaki can assume the form of insects when it serves their purpose.

III.

Grotesque as these beliefs now seem to us, it was not unnatural that ancient Eastern fancy should associate insects with ghosts and devils. In our visible world there are no other creatures so wonderful and so mysterious; and the true history of certain insects actually realises the dreams of mythology. To the minds of primitive men, the mere facts of insect-metamorphosis must have seemed uncanny; and what but goblinry or magic could account for the monstrous existence of beings so similar to dead leaves, or to flowers, or to joints of grass, that the keenest human sight could detect their presence only when they began

Gaki

to walk or to fly? Even for the entomologist of to-day, insects remain the most incomprehensible of creatures. We have learned from him that they must be acknowledged "the most successful of organised beings" in the battle for existence;—that the delicacy and the complexity of their structures surpass anything ever imagined of marvellous before the age of the microscope;—that their senses so far exceed our own in refinement as to prove us deaf and blind by comparison. Nevertheless, the insect world remains a world of hopeless enigmas. Who can explain for us the mystery of the eyes of a myriad facets, or the secret of the ocular brains connected with them? Do those astounding eyes perceive the ultimate structure of matter? does their vision pierce opacity, after the manner of the Roëntgen rays? (Or how interpret the deadly aim of that ichneumon-fly which plunges its ovipositor through solid wood to reach the grub embedded in the grain?) What, again, of those marvellous ears in breasts and thighs and knees and feet—ears that hear sounds beyond the limit of human audition? and what of the musical structures evolved to produce such fairy melody? What of the ghostly feet that walk upon flowing water? What of the chemistry that kindles the fire-fly's lamp—making the cold and beautiful light that all our electric science cannot imitate? And those newly discovered, incomparably delicate organs for which we have yet no name, because our wisest cannot decide the nature of them—do they really, as some would suggest, keep the insect-mind informed of things unknown to human sense—visibilities of magnetism, odours of light, tastes of sound? . . . Even the little that we have been able to learn about insects fills us with the wonder that is akin to fear. The lips that are hands, and the horns that are eyes, and the tongues that are drills; the multiple devilish mouths that move in four ways at once; the living scissors and saws and boring-pumps and brace-bits; the exquisite elfish weapons which no human skill can copy, even in the finest watch-spring steel—what superstition of old ever dreamed of sights like these? Indeed, all that nightmare ever conceived of faceless horror, and all that ecstasy ever imagined of phantasmal pulchritude, can appear but vapid and void by comparison with the stupefying facts of entomology. But there is something spectral, something alarming, in the very beauty of insects . . .

IV.

Whether gaki do or do not exist, there is at least some shadowing of truth in the Eastern belief that the dead become insects. Undoubtedly our human dust must help, over and over again for millions of ages, to build up numberless weird shapes of life. But as to that question of my revery under the pine-trees—whether present acts and thoughts can have anything to do with the future distribution and re-quickening of that dust—whether human conduct can of itself predetermine the shapes into which human atoms will be recast—no reply is possible. I doubt—but I do not know. Neither does anybody else.

Supposing, however, that the order of the universe were really as Buddhists believe, and that I knew myself foredoomed, by reason of stupidities in this existence, to live hereafter the life of an insect, I am not sure that the prospect would frighten me. There are insects of which it is difficult to think with equanimity; but the state of an independent, highly organised, respectable insect could not be so very bad. I should even look forward, with some pleasurable curiosity, to any chance of viewing the world through the marvellous compound eyes of a beetle, an ephemera, or a dragon-fly. As an ephemera, indeed, I might enjoy the possession of three different kinds of eyes, and the power to see colours now totally unimaginable. Estimated in degrees of human time, my life would be short—a single summer day would include the best part of it; but to ephemeral consciousness a few minutes would appear a season; and my one day of winged existence—barring possible mishaps—would be one unwearied joy of dancing in golden air. And I could feel in my winged state neither hunger nor thirst—having no real mouth or stomach: I should be, in very truth, a wind-eater . . . Nor should I fear to enter upon the much less ethereal condition of a dragon-fly. I should then have to bear carnivorous hunger, and to hunt a great deal; but even dragon-flies, after the fierce joy of the chase, can indulge themselves in solitary meditation. Besides, what wings would then be mine!—and what eyes! . . .

I could pleasurably anticipate even the certainty of becoming an *amembō*,[4] and so being able to run and to slide upon water—though children might catch me, and bite off my long fine legs. But I think that I should better enjoy the existence of a *sémi*—a large and lazy cicada, basking on wind-rocked trees, sipping only dew, and singing from dawn till dusk. Of course there would be perils to encounter—danger from hawks and crows and sparrows—danger from insects of prey—danger from bamboos tipped with birdlime by naughty little boys. But in every condition of life there must be risks; and in spite of the risks, I imagine that Anacreon uttered little more than the truth, in his praise of the cicada: "O thou earth-born—song-loving—free from pain—having flesh without blood—thou art nearly equal to the Gods!" . . . In fact I have not been able to convince myself that it is really an inestimable privilege to be reborn a human being. And if the thinking of this thought, and the act of writing it down, must inevitably affect my next rebirth, then let me hope that the state to which I am destined will not be worse than that of a cicada or of a dragon-fly;—climbing the cryptomerias to clash my tiny cymbals in the sun—or haunting, with soundless flicker of amethyst and gold, some holy silence of lotus-pools.

Notes

[1] The word "*gaki*" is the Japanese Buddhist rendering of the Sanscrit term "*preta*", signifying a spirit in that circle or state of torment called the World of Hungry Ghosts.

[2] Abridged from the *Shōbō-nen-jō-Kyō*. A full translation of the extraordinary chapter relating to the gaki would try the reader's nerves rather severely.

[3] The following story of a tree-spirit is typical: In the garden of a Samurai named Satsuma Shichizaēmon, who lived in the village of Echigawa in the province of Omi, there was a very old énoki. (The énoki, or "*Celtis chinensis*", is commonly thought to be a goblin-tree.) From ancient times the ancestors of the family had been careful never to cut a branch of this tree or to remove any of its leaves. But Shichizaēmon, who was very self-willed, one day announced that he intended to have the tree cut down. During the following night a monstrous being appeared to the mother of Shichizaēmon, in a dream, and told her that if the énoki were cut down, every member of the household should die. But when this warning was communicated to Shichizaēmon, he only laughed; and he then sent a man to cut down the tree. No sooner had it been cut down than Shichizaēmon became violently insane. For several days he remained furiously mad, crying out at intervals,

Gaki

"The tree! the tree! the tree!" He said that the tree put out its branches, like hands, to tear him. In this condition he died. Soon afterward his wife went mad, crying out that the tree was killing her; and she died screaming with fear. One after another, all the people in that house, not excepting the servants, went mad and died. The dwelling long remained unoccupied thereafter, no one daring even to enter the garden. At last it was remembered that before these things happened a daughter of the Satsuma family had become a Buddhist nun, and that she was still living, under the name of Jikun, in a temple at Yamashirō. This nun was sent for; and by request of the villagers she took up her residence in the house, where she continued to live until the time of her death,—daily reciting a special service on behalf of the spirit that had dwelt in the tree. From the time that she began to live in the house the tree-spirit ceased to give trouble. This story is related on the authority of the priest Shungyō, who said that he had heard it from the lips of the nun herself.

[4] A water-insect, resembling what we call a "skater". In some parts of the country it is said that the boy who wants to become a good swimmer must eat the legs of an *amembō*.

安芸之介の夢
The Dream of Akinosuké

In the district called Toīchi of Yamato province, there used to live a *gōshi* named Miyata Akinosuké . . . (Here I must tell you that in Japanese feudal times there was a privileged class of soldier-farmers,—free-holders,—corresponding to the class of yeomen in England; and these were called *gōshi*.)

In Akinosuké's garden there was a great and ancient cedar-tree, under which he was wont to rest on sultry days. One very warm afternoon he was sitting under this tree with two of his friends, fellow-*gōshi*, chatting and drinking wine, when he felt all of a sudden very drowsy,—so drowsy that he begged his friends to excuse him for taking a nap in their presence. Then he lay down at the foot of the tree, and dreamed this dream:—

He thought that as he was lying there in his garden, he saw a procession, like the train of some great *daimyō*, descending a hill near by, and that he got up to look at it. A very grand procession it proved to be,—more imposing than anything of the kind which he had ever seen before; and it was advancing toward his dwelling. He observed in the van of it a number of young men richly apparelled, who were drawing a great lacquered palace-carriage, or *gosho-guruma*, hung with bright blue silk. When the procession arrived within a short distance of the house it halted; and a richly dressed man—evidently a person of

The Dream of Akinosuké

rank—advanced from it, approached Akinosuké, bowed to him profoundly, and then said:—

"Honoured sir, you see before you *kérai* (vassal) of the Kokūo of Tokoyo.[1] My master, the King, commands me to greet you in his august name, and to place myself wholly at your disposal. He also bids me inform you that he augustly desires your presence at the palace. Be therefore pleased immediately to enter this honourable carriage, which he has sent for your conveyance."

Upon hearing these words Akinosuké wanted to make some fitting reply; but he was too much astonished and embarrassed for speech;—and in the same moment his will seemed to melt away from him, so that he could only do as the *kérai* bade him. He entered the carriage; the *kérai* took a place beside him, and made a signal; the drawers, seizing the silken ropes, turned the great vehicle southward;—and the journey began.

In a very short time, to Akinosuké's amazement, the carriage stopped in front of a huge two-storied gateway (*rōmon*), of Chinese style, which he had never before seen. Here the *kérai* dismounted, saying, "I go to announce the honourable arrival,"—and he disappeared. After some little waiting, Akinosuké saw two noble-looking men, wearing robes of purple silk and high caps of the form indicating lofty rank, come from the gateway. These, after having respectfully saluted him, helped him to descend from the carriage, and led him through the great gate and across a vast garden, to the entrance of a palace whose front appeared to extend, west and east, to a distance of miles. Akinosuké was then shown into a reception-room of wonderful size and splendour. His guides conducted him to the place of honour, and respectfully seated themselves apart; while serving-maids, in costume of ceremony, brought refreshments. When Akinosuké had partaken of the refreshments, the two purple-robed attendants bowed low before him, and addressed him in the following words,—each speaking alternately, according to the etiquette of courts:—

"It is now our honourable duty to inform you . . . as to the reason of your having been summoned hither . . . Our master, the King, augustly desires that you become his son-in-law; . . . and it is his wish and command that you shall wed this very day . . . the August Princess, his maiden-daughter . . . We shall soon conduct you to the presence-chamber . . . where His Augustness even now is waiting to receive you . . . But it will be necessary that we first invest you . . . with the appropriate garments of ceremony."[2]

Having thus spoken, the attendants rose together, and proceeded to an alcove containing a great chest of gold lacquer. They opened the chest, and took from it various robes and girdles of rich material, and a *kamuri*, or regal headdress. With these they attired Akinosuké as befitted a princely bridegroom; and he was then conducted to the presence-room, where he saw the Kokūo of Tokoyo seated upon the *daiza*,[3] wearing the high black cap of state, and robed in robes of yellow silk. Before the *daiza*, to left and right, a multitude of dignitaries sat in rank, motionless and splendid as images in a temple; and Akinosuké, advancing into their midst, saluted the king with the triple prostration of usage. The king greeted him with gracious words, and then said:—

"You have already been informed as to the reason of your having been summoned to Our presence. We have decided that you shall become the adopted husband of Our only daughter;—and the wedding ceremony shall now be performed."

As the king finished speaking, a sound of joyful music was heard; and a long train of beautiful court ladies ad-

The Dream of Akinosuké

vanced from behind a curtain, to conduct Akinosuké to the room in which his bride awaited him.

The room was immense; but it could scarcely contain the multitude of guests assembled to witness the wedding ceremony. All bowed down before Akinosuké as he took his place, facing the King's daughter, on the kneeling-cushion prepared for him. As a maiden of heaven the bride appeared to be; and her robes were beautiful as a summer sky. And the marriage was performed amid great rejoicing.

Afterwards the pair were conducted to a suite of apartments that had been prepared for them in another portion of the palace; and there they received the congratulations of many noble persons, and wedding gifts beyond counting.

Some days later Akinosuké was again summoned to the throne-room. On this occasion he was received even more graciously than before; and the King said to him:—

"In the southwestern part of Our dominion there is an island called Raishū. We have now appointed you Governor of that island. You will find the people loyal and docile; but their laws have not yet been brought into proper accord with the laws of Tokoyo; and their customs have not been properly regulated. We entrust you with the duty of improving their social condition as far as may be possible; and We desire that you shall rule them with kindness and wisdom. All preparations necessary for your journey to Raishū have already been made."

So Akinosuké and his bride departed from the palace of Tokoyo, accompanied to the shore by a great escort of nobles and officials; and they embarked upon a ship of state provided by the king. And with favouring winds they safely sailed to Raishū, and found the good people of that island assembled upon the beach to welcome them.

Akinosuké entered at once upon his new duties; and they did not prove to be hard. During the first three years of his governorship he was occupied chiefly with the framing and the enactment of laws; but he had wise counsellors to help him, and he never found the work unpleasant. When it was all finished, he had no active duties to perform, beyond attending the rites and ceremonies ordained by ancient custom. The country was so healthy and so fertile that sickness and want were unknown; and the people were so good that no laws were ever broken. And Akinosuké dwelt and ruled in Raishū for twenty years more,—making in all twenty-three years of sojourn, during which no shadow of sorrow traversed his life.

But in the twenty-fourth year of his governorship, a great misfortune came upon him; for his wife, who had borne him seven children,—five boys and two girls,—fell sick and died. She was buried, with high pomp, on the summit of a beautiful hill in the district of Hanryōkō; and a monument, exceedingly splendid, was placed above her grave. But Akinosuké felt such grief at her death that he no longer cared to live.

Now when the legal period of mourning was over, there came to Raishū, from the Tokoyo palace, a *shisha*, or royal messenger. The *shisha* delivered to Akinosuké a message of condolence, and then said to him:—

"These are the words which our august master, the King of Tokoyo, commands that I repeat to you: 'We will now send you back to your own people and country. As for the seven children, they are the grandsons and the granddaughters of the King, and shall be fitly cared for. Do not, therefore, allow your mind to be troubled concerning them.' "

The Dream of Akinosuké

On receiving this mandate, Akinosuké submissively prepared for his departure. When all his affairs had been settled, and the ceremony of bidding farewell to his counsellors and trusted officials had been concluded, he was escorted with much honour to the port. There he embarked upon the ship sent for him; and the ship sailed out into the blue sea, under the blue sky; and the shape of the island of Raishū itself turned blue, and then turned grey, and then vanished forever . . . And Akinosuké suddenly awoke—under the cedar tree in his own garden! . . .

For the moment he was stupefied and dazed. But he perceived his two friends still seated near him,—drinking and chatting merrily. He stared at them in a bewildered way, and cried aloud,—

"How strange!"

"Akinosuké must have been dreaming," one of them exclaimed, with a laugh. "What did you see, Akinosuké, that was strange?"

Then Akinosuké told his dream,—that dream of three-and-twenty years' sojourn in the realm of Tokoyo, in the island of Raishū;—and they were astonished, because he had really slept for no more than a few minutes.

One *gōshi* said:— -

"Indeed, you saw strange things. We also saw something strange while you were napping. A little yellow butterfly was fluttering over your face for a moment or two; and we watched it. Then it alighted on the ground beside you, close to the tree; and almost as soon as it alighted there, a big, big ant came out of a hole, and seized it and pulled it down into the hole. Just before you woke up, we saw that very butterfly come out of the hole again, and flutter over your face as before. And then it suddenly disappeared: we do not know where it went."

"Perhaps it was Akinosuké's soul," the other *gōshi* said;—"certainly I thought I saw it fly into his mouth . . . But, even if that butterfly *was* Akinosuké's soul, the fact would not explain his dream."

"The ants might explain it," returned the first speaker. "Ants are queer beings—possibly goblins . . . Anyhow, there is a big ants' nest under that cedar tree." . . .

"Let us look!" cried Akinosuké, greatly moved by this suggestion. And he went for a spade.

The ground about and beneath the cedar-tree proved to have been excavated, in a most surprising way, by a prodigious colony of ants. The ants had furthermore built inside their excavations; and their tiny constructions of straw, clay, and stems bore an odd resemblance to miniature towns. In the middle of a structure considerably larger than the rest there was a marvellous swarming of small ants around the body of one very big ant, which had yellowish wings and a long black head.

"Why, there is the King of my dream!" said Akinosuké; "and there is the palace of Tokoyo! How extraordinary! . . . Raishū ought to lie somewhere southwest of it—to the left of that big root . . . Yes!—here it is! . . . How very strange! Now I am sure that I can find the mountain of Hanryōkō, and the grave of the princess." . . .

In the wreck of the nest he searched and searched, and at last discovered a tiny mound, on the top of which was fixed a water-worn pebble, in shape resembling a Buddhist monument. Underneath it he found—embedded in clay—the dead body of a female ant.

Notes

[1] This name "Tokoyo" is indefinite. According to circumstances it may signify any unknown country,—or

that undiscovered country from whose bourn no traveller returns,—or that Fairyland of far-eastern fable, the Realm of Hōrai. The term "*Kokūō*" means the ruler of a country,—therefore a king. The original phrase, *Tokoyo no Kokūō* might be rendered here as "the Ruler of Hōrai", or "the King of Fairyland".

[2] The last phrase, according to old custom, had to be uttered by both attendants at the same time. All these ceremonial observances can still be studied on the Japanese stage.

[3] This was the name given to the estrade, or dais, upon which a feudal prince or ruler sat in state. The term literally signifies "great seat".

謝辞
Acknowledgements

Insect Literature was first published by Hokuseidō Press, Tōkyō (1921). The publisher would like to thank the following people for their assistance in the publication of this new edition: Anne-Sylvie Homassel for her introduction to and initiation of this project; Rebecca Bourke and Edward Crandall for their Japanese translations; John Moran for his expertise in all things Hearn; Takato Yamamoto for his artwork and Mayumi Kubota of Uptight Co. Ltd. for arranging for its use; Yaeko Crandall for her calligraphy; and finally Xand Lourenco, Jim Rockhill, Meggan Kehrli, and Ken Mackenzie for their help with design and preparation of the text.

༄

"Butterflies" first appeared in *Kwaidan* (Boston & New York: Houghton, Mifflin & Co., 1904)

"Mosquitoes" first appeared in *Kwaidan* (Boston & New York: Houghton, Mifflin & Co., 1904)

"Ants" first appeared in *Kwaidan* (Boston & New York: Houghton, Mifflin & Co., 1904)

Acknowledgements

"Story of a Fly" first appeared in *Kottō* (London & New York: Macmillan & Co., 1902)

"Fireflies" first appeared in *Kottō* (London & New York: Macmillan & Co., 1902)

"Dragon-flies" first appeared in *A Japanese Miscellany* (Boston: Little, Brown & Co., 1901)

"Sémi" first appeared in *Shadowings* (Boston: Little, Brown & Co., 1900)

"Insect-Musicians" first appeared in *Exotics and Retrospectives* (Boston: Little, Brown & Co., 1898)

"Kusa-hibari" first appeared in *Kottō* (London & New York: Macmillan & Co., 1902)

"Some Poems about Insects" first appeared in *Interpretation of Literature* (New York: Dodd, Mead & Co., 1915)

"Insects and Greek Poetry" first appeared in the *Atlantic Monthly*, May 1847. It was first collected in 1926 (New York: William Edwin Rudge)

"Some French Poems about Insects" first appeared in *Life and Literature* (New York: Dodd, Mead & Co., 1917)

"Insect Politics" first appeared in the *New Orleans Item*, 11 July 1878. It was first collected in *Editorials* (Boston & New York: Houghton, Mifflin & Co., 1926)

Insect Literature

"Under the Electric Light" first appeared in the *Daily City Item*, 6 August 1880. It was first collected in *Inventing New Orleans* (Jackson: University Press of Mississippi, 2001)

"——! ——!! Mosquitoes!!!" first appeared in the *Daily City Item*, 28 July 1880. It was first collected in *Inventing New Orleans* (Jackson: University Press of Mississippi, 2001)

"The Festive" first appeared in the *Daily City Item*, 13 October 1880. It was first collected in Inventing New Orleans (Jackson: University Press of Mississippi, 2001)

"The Jewel Insect" first appeared in *Re-Echo* by Kazuo Hearn Koizumi (Caldwell: The Caxton Printers, 1957). Noted as "Perhaps Hearn's creation".

"Dr. Hava's Tarantula" first appeared in the *New Orleans Item*, 4 May 1881. It was first collected in *The New Radiance and Other Essays* (Tōkyō: Hokuseido Press, 1939)

"Gaki" first appeared in *Kottō* (London & New York: Macmillan & Co., 1902)

"The Dream of Akinosuké" first appeared in *Kwaidan* (Boston & New York: Houghton Mifflin & Co., 1904)

The illustrations on the full-title page and page 130 are from *Exotics and Retrospectives* (Boston: Little, Brown & Co., 1898); the illustrations on pages 42, 46, 158, and 249 are by Genjiro Yeto and appeared in *Kottō* (London & New York: Macmillan & Co., 1902); the illustration on page 72 is from *A Japanese Miscellany* (Boston: Little, Brown & Co., 1901); and the illustration from page 104 is from *Shadowings* (Boston: Little, Brown & Co., 1900).

著者について
About the Author

Born on the Greek island of Lefkada, Lafcadio Hearn (1850-1904) was brought up in both Ireland and England. At nineteen he emigrated to the United States where he became a journalist. After a sojourn in the French West Indies, he sailed for Japan in 1890. Hearn wrote extensively about his new homeland, its tales, customs, and religions, acting as a bridge between Japan and the Western world. He died in Tokyo where he is buried under his Japanese name, Koizumi Yakumo. His notable books include *Glimpses of Unfamiliar Japan* (1894), *In Ghostly Japan* (1899), *Shadowings* (1900), and *Kwaidan* (1904).

SWAN RIVER PRESS

Founded in 2003, Swan River Press is an independent publishing company, based in Dublin, Ireland, dedicated to gothic, supernatural, and fantastic literature. We specialise in limited edition hardbacks, publishing fiction from around the world with an emphasis on Ireland's contributions to the genre.

www.swanriverpress.ie

*"Handsome, beautifully made volumes . . .
altogether irresistible."*

– Michael Dirda, *Washington Post*

*"It [is] often down to small, independent, specialist presses
to keep the candle of horror fiction flickering . . . "*

– Darryl Jones, *Irish Times*

"Swan River Press has emerged as one of the most inspiring new presses over the past decade. Not only are the books beautifully presented and professionally produced, but they aspire consistently to high literary quality and originality, ranging from current writers of supernatural/weird fiction to rare or forgotten works by departed authors."

– Peter Bell, *Ghosts & Scholars*

THE GREEN BOOK
*Writings on Irish Gothic,
Supernatural and Fantastic Literature*

edited by
Brian J. Showers

Aimed at a general readership and published twice-yearly, *The Green Book* features commentaries, articles, and reviews on Irish Gothic, Supernatural and Fantastic literature.

Certainly favourites such as Bram Stoker and John Connolly will come to mind, but *The Green Book* also showcases Ireland's other notable fantasists: Fitz-James O'Brien, Charlotte Riddell, Lafcadio Hearn, Rosa Mulholland, J. Sheridan Le Fanu, Cheiro, Harry Clarke, Dorothy Macardle, Lord Dunsany, Elizabeth Bowen, C. S. Lewis, Mervyn Wall, Conor McPherson . . . and many others.

"*A welcome addition to the realm of accessible
nonfiction about supernatural horror.*"

– Ellen Datlow

"*Eminently readable . . . [an] engaging little journal
that treads the path between accessibility and
academic depth with real panache.*"

– Peter Tenant, *Black Static*

STRANGE EPIPHANIES

Peter Bell

A mentally disturbed woman is entrapped in Beltane rituals in the Cumbrian fells; a widower mourning his wife falls beneath the mystic allure of Iona; a quest to the Italian Apennines brings a lonely man to a dread Marian revelation; an alcoholic on a Scottish isle is haunted by a deceased chronicler of local legend; in a small German town a sinister doll discloses truths about a murky family tragedy; an unknown journal by a Victorian travel-writer sends a woman on a grim odyssey to Transylvania; in a childhood holiday paradise a man encounters a demented artist's terrifying legacy. The protagonists in Peter Bell's stories confront the awesome, the numinous, the uncanny, the lure of genius loci, and landscapes undergoing strange epiphanies.

"Bell is not a purveyor of pure horror, but of something much more interesting . . . Bell's world is shot through with strange beauty but full of tragic and alarming occurrences."

– Wormwood

"A Dazzling Collection of Weird Fiction Gems . . . All the stories in Strange Epiphanies are virtually pitch perfect."

– Dead Reckonings

GREEN TEA

J. Sheridan Le Fanu

Published alongside "Carmilla" in the landmark collection *In a Glass Darkly* (1872), Le Fanu's "Green Tea" was first serialised in Charles Dickens' magazine *All the Year Round* in 1869. Since its first publication, Le Fanu's tale has lost none of its potency. "Green Tea" tells of the good natured Reverend Jennings, who writes late at night on arcane topics abetted by a steady supply of green tea. Is he insane or have these nocturnal activities opened an "interior sight" that affords a route of entry for an increasingly malignant simian companion? This 150th anniversary edition of "Green Tea", with illustrations by Alisdair Wood and an introduction by Matthew Holness, is the definitive celebration of Le Fanu's masterpiece of psychological terror and despair.

"Even 150 years after it was published,
'Green Tea' has stood firmly against the test of time as a
wonderfully eerie and well-crafted ghost story."

– *Ghosts & Scholars*

"To paraphrase Little Women, it wouldn't be Christmas
without any ghost stories . . . Swan River Press
has just issued a beautiful keepsake volume of
J. Sheridan Le Fanu's Green Tea."

– Michael Dirda, *Washington Post*

www.ingramcontent.com/pod-product-compliance
Lightning Source LLC
Chambersburg PA
CBHW020902080526
44589CB00011B/399